COLONY KIDS

COLONY KIDS

Adventures of the First Year in Alaska

Heather Cooper Lehe

PO Box 221974 Anchorage, Alaska 99522-1974
books@publicationconsultants.com
www.publicationconsultants.com

ISBN 978-1-59433-265-4
eBook ISBN 978-1-59433-266-1
Library of Congress Catalog Card Number: 2011944735

Manufactured in the United States of America.

Dedication

Colony Kids is dedicated to my Grandma, Margaret Welsh, whose adventurous spirit left an indelible mark on my life.

Contents

Acknowledgements

Many people were involved in the research for this book. I would especially like to thank the following *colony kids* whom I had the immense privilege of interviewing:

Lawrence Vasanoja, Maralyn (Vasanoja) Hartley, Wayne Bouwens, Laura (France) Stenberg, Beverly (Larsh) Hayes, Lorraine (McKechnie) Herman, JoeAnn (Lentz) Vanover, and Lynn Sandvik. Maralyn Hartley actually lent me her daily diary that started January 1, 1936, and whose daily observations and notes brought the day-to-day experiences of that first year to life. Others who shared memories and valuable tidbits in passing include: Gerry (Kindgren) Keeling, Dorothy (Vasanoja) Hildre, Helen (Havemeister) Riley, Jackie (Smith) Cabo, Pearl (Vasanoja) Jensen, Don Dinkel, Gail (Eckert) Roland, Arlene (Benson) Fox, and some I, regrettably, failed to note as I inquired about life as a colonist even before I thought about writing a book. I also regret that I could not interview all surviving colony kids old enough to remember that first year.

Others who eagerly shared their knowledge, insight, and passion for the rich history of the Matanuska Valley include Palmer Mayor Delena Johnson, then of the Palmer Museum who gave me a walking tour of Palmer, including crawling through holes in fences, to point out historical locations and events, and Lorie Kirker and Lynette Lehn, of Alaskana Books, who lent me one-of-a-kind books for my research. Information was also gathered from the Palmer Museum,

The Palmer Historical Society's Colony House Museum, Palmer Library, the Colonist Monument in Palmer, and the Seward Museum.

Though historical fiction, I have tried to incorporate and stay true to as many stories as possible. Where the topic was a sensitive one, I have changed the names or specific events of those involved. Others I have kept with their true identity and hope the story brings honor to their memory. Though the main characters portray many of the stories shared by colony kids, they are purely fictitious and any resemblance to a real person is coincidental.

Of course, this book would not have been written without the encouragement and continued support from my ever-faithful husband, Tom, my children, Tommy, Doug, Anna, and Lauren, and my dear friend, Wendy Strohmeyer. Their willingness to proofread, edit, comment, and keep me going will be forever appreciated.

It is my sincere hope and desire that this book will reveal to all who read it, especially young people, a better understanding and appreciation for those who had the courage and resolve to leave families and forge a new life with so many unknowns, so far away. Though a few books have been written from the perspective of the adults, little is found about the children's experiences. In 1935, on a journey that took more than two weeks to complete and with a one-way ticket in hand, families gave up everything for the possibility of a better life despite the guarantee of hardships, usually with several children in tow. The more I learn about these determined, rugged, optimistic people, the more impressed I become. The families who stayed and helped make the Matanuska Valley the thriving community it has become are truly amazing. If you know of, or are related to, a colony kid, please ask them to share their story!

Chapter 1
Fire!

Something wet licked Paul's face. He had been dreaming of deer hunting with his pa and grandpa, sitting beside the campfire. Thick smoke swirled around them.

Again, something licked his face and nudged his arm.

"Rascal, what …," he awoke in a daze, coughing. Smoke filled the room. The dog sat by the bed, whining as she pawed at Paul with one foot. Paul suddenly realized it wasn't a dream.

"Ma, Clara, Minnie! Wake up! We gotta get out of here—the house is on fire! Hurry!" Paul yelled frantically. His heart beat wildly in his chest. It was hard to breathe. "Ma! Get the girls!"

No one answered.

Crawling under the smoke, he cried out in desperation as he tried to push Ma's door open. He coughed and gasped for air as he felt for her and frantically shook her. *Why won't she wake up?* His throat burned.

"Paul? What's happening?" she finally sputtered and gasped. Smoke filled the room.

"The house is on fire! We need to get the girls out!" he yelled hoarsely.

Both crawled to the girls' room and pulled them out of their beds and out the door. They groaned and coughed, but weren't fully awake until they were outside in the cool night air. Clara started to sob.

"Oh, honey," Ma hugged both girls tight and rocked back and forth to console them. "Everything's gonna be alright."

"Where's Rascal?" Paul looked around. His blue eyes were bloodshot from the smoke, his shirt was torn.

"Don't go back in there, Paul," pleaded Ma. "It's too late!"

But Paul wouldn't listen. He made his way back to the house and opened the door, calling Rascal's name over and over. There was no sign of her. The heat was unbearable. Finally, he turned and stumbled away from the house, hardly able to breathe.

"Paul, look!" Ma shouted.

A scraggly brown dog had crawled on her belly to the door, whining. Paul tried to run back to the house but his legs were weak and he fell several times. Using every ounce of strength, he reached Rascal and carried her back to Ma and the girls, collapsing on the ground with the dog in his arms. She licked his face weakly.

"She woke me up," Paul's voice cracked. "I just couldn't let her die."

In shock, they watched the little ramshackle house as it was devoured in flames and the walls began to fall in on each other. Ma sobbed and hugged her children hard.

Everything was lost.

"We're all safe, thank the Lord. Oh Pa, why aren't you here?" she cried. "And my piano ..." Ma muttered sadly.

"My beautiful piano."

———

The tall, lanky man stood with his thumbs hooked in his suspenders, his shoulders slumped sadly as he surveyed what had been his home. Four days had gone by since the fire. All that remained was a pile of ashes and a skeleton of bricks that had been the fireplace.

"I was wonderin' when you'd be comin' home, Henry. Sorry you had to come back to this," his neighbor patted him on the back. "At least Mary and the kids are safe at her folks' place, like I said."

"Where'd the animals go?"

"Paul and I done took 'em over there. The ewe was due to have her lamb any day—reckon that happened while you were away."

"Lord, what next?" Pa sighed. "Well, at least everyone's safe. Guess it never was much of a house anyway," Pa mumbled under his breath. "Thanks for all your help, Virgil." Pa finally turned away from the house. "Better head over there and try to come up with something. Sure ain't a good time to lose your home, if there ever was a good time."

"Nope, this here Depression, as they call it, has been pretty tough on us all. No work, no food, no nothin'. I'm sure sorry 'bout yer house, though. That's a real bad deal. Maybe the government can help in some way."

"Naw," Pa answered angrily as he got in the truck and slammed the door. "Can't stand havin' to ask for help as it is, but got to feed the family somehow. Well, see ya 'round." He gave a nod of his head as he backed the truck out of the driveway and headed for his in-laws' place, ten miles away. When Pa came to the intersection he hesitated for several minutes, then turned in the opposite the direction of his family.

A few hours later Pa pulled into Gramps' and Gran's driveway. Minnie and Clara, who had been playing with Rascal, raced to meet him. Ma ran out of the house with Gran, while Paul and Gramps came out of the barn.

"Am I ever glad to see you!" Pa's voice was full of emotion as he picked both girls up and hugged them hard. "Got here as fast as I could. Just saw the house. Unbelievable. Wish I'd a been here."

Ma joined the circle and started crying into Pa's shoulder.

Paul stood quietly, his hands in his pockets. It wasn't proper for men to show emotion. But Ma, who was now crying and laughing at the same time, reached out and grabbed him and the five of them hugged each other for a long time.

Finally Pa let go, and stepped back.

"When they told me about the fire I about went crazy wonderin' if you were all okay," Pa said as he blew his nose into his handkerchief. "Hate bein' away from you all."

Pa's actually gettin' choked up, Paul thought. *Ain't never seen him do that before.*

"Guess what, Pa! Did you know Wosy had her lamb?" five-year-old Clara tugged on his sleeve.

"Really?" Pa acted surprised. "I bet it's cute!"

"Oh, she's the sweetest little thing!" Minnie exclaimed. "And I'm eight now," she announced proudly.

"Yep, we had a birthday while you were gone." Ma finally spoke, dabbing her eyes with a hankie. "And Paul's been a big help."

"Hey there, son. Thanks for keepin' things goin' while I was away. That's my boy." Pa tousled Paul's hair and slapped him on the back, affectionately but hard. Paul winced. "Don't know what I'd do without ya."

Paul looked down at his feet, embarrassed and proud at the same time.

Pa shook Gramps' hand and gave Gran a quick hug. He had a hard time showing them how grateful he was for their help.

He turned to Paul, Minnie, and Clara. "If you all don't mind, I've got something pretty important to discuss with Ma."

"Come on, girls," said Gran. "Gramps and I'll take you for a little walk down to the creek."

"I'll finish the chores," said Paul. He glanced at Ma but it was obvious she had no idea what Pa wanted to talk about.

They went into the house and Paul started for the barn, but only walked partway. *What could they be discussin'?* Hiding behind the screen door, he listened to their conversation.

"Well, Mary, things are pretty desperate now, without a home and all. So I stopped by the county office before headin' out here. Figured there might be some sort of assistance for rebuildin' the house, or maybe they had another place we could rent for a while." He looked at Ma.

She handed him a cup of coffee and nodded for him to continue.

"Well, come to find out, the lady there told me …"

Suddenly Rascal started barking wildly and Paul couldn't hear what Pa was saying. He turned to see Daisy, the cow, trotting out the barn door and along the path to the back field. Rascal barked at her heels.

Dang! I better go git Daisy. But what did Pa say? What did the lady tell him? He put his ear back toward the door.

"But Henry, will I ever see my folks again? That's so far away," Ma sniffled.

Far away? Ever see Gramps and Gran again? Uh oh, that don't sound good.

"I know, Mary, but what's left for us here?" Pa stood looking out the window in his worn dungarees and plaid flannel shirt. His face looked tired and worn.

"Things are bad in Minnesota, and on top of that we don't even have a home!"

He hit his fist on the window frame. "I'm gone all the time and

I still can't find work. Nothin' grows in the fields with dust storms and no rain. It's been over two years!" He turned back to Ma, his voice a little softer. "I know it's far away. But it's a chance for us to start over and make a go of it. I hate this Depression, or whatever they call it! I hate takin' the government's money, but this is an unbelievable opportunity!"

There was an uncomfortable silence.

Paul held his breath. *Maybe it's something good after all.*

"Do we have to decide so soon? The kids are still in school and Paul just turned thirteen. That's a hard age to leave your friends. And we have so much to do to get ready …" Her voice trailed off as if she knew it was no use. When Pa made up his mind there was no changing it. "Well, give me a couple of hours to get used to the idea, and we'll let the kids know at supper."

Dang, I can't tell if it's good or bad!

Ma pushed her chair back to get up and Paul knew the conversation was over. He quietly tiptoed toward the back field to catch Daisy and get started on the chores.

It took a half hour to catch the cow, even with Gramps helping.

The lamb born the day before baaed softly as it tottered around the pen. Paul threw some hay in the corner for Rosy and laughed as he watched the lamb nuzzle its mother for milk. After filling the chicken feeder with mash and giving the hens some water, he put seven eggs into a basket to be washed for breakfast. Rascal lay beside the stool as Paul sat down to milk Daisy.

Sure wonder what Pa has up his sleeve. Where in the world is he thinkin' to move to? Kinda excitin'!

Deep in thought, Paul didn't notice the fly land on Daisy's belly. She kicked at it with her back leg, which sent the bucket of milk flying.

"Dangit, Daisy! Now I gotta start over!" he muttered. "Guess I'd better pay attention."

Finally done, he watched as steam from the warm milk rose gently from the bucket. Paul leaned back against a bale of hay and chewed thoughtfully on a piece of straw as Rascal scratched her ear, stretched, and lay her head on his stomach. He stroked her head and looked around. Shafts of light came in through the barn walls and lit up tiny particles of chaff that swirled in the air. Flies buzzed and pigeons cooed softly in the rafters overhead.

"Love bein' in a barn, don't you ol' girl?" he scratched her behind the ears. "It's peaceful, and no one bothers us. If we move, there better be a barn."

His parents' conversation kept replaying in his mind. *Where could we possibly go? I know we don't have any money. Without the government helping we wouldn't even have food to eat, just like all our neighbors. What does Pa mean it's an unbelievable opportunity?* He couldn't wait to go in for supper to find out.

Chapter 2
A Cold Barren Land

Alaska! Paul almost choked on his food when Pa told the family the news at dinner.

"Where in the world is Alaska?" he sputtered. "Isn't that way up north where it's cold and snowy all the time?"

"Here," said Ma, still sniffling as she carried Gran's old encyclopedia in from the living room. "I had to look it up myself, though I'm not sure I like what it says."

The one small picture showed a little log cabin with a sod roof standing in a clearing. Snow-covered mountains towered in the background. An odd assortment of tools, rusted traps, and animal pelts hung on the outside wall, while a thin ribbon of smoke rose from the crooked chimney pipe.

Pa took the book from Ma and read a paragraph. "Alaska was purchased from Russia in 1867 for $7.2 million. This U.S. Territory is home to Native Indians, Eskimos, and Aleuts, and a few hardy trappers who somehow manage to survive in a cold, barren land."

Tears rolled down Ma's cheeks again.

"Is that really where we're gonna move to, Pa?" Paul couldn't believe it.

"Well, the government's givin' a few folks like us the chance to move to Alaska. That book is ancient and outdated." He set it aside. "A lady from the county said it's farmin' country, and they're gonna build folks a house and barn and help 'em get started with a new life.

Course it ain't all free. It's got to be paid back. She said the vegetables are huge up there! And there's all kinds of huntin' and fishin', and even a city not too far away." He looked over at Ma who was about to cry again. He quickly turned back to Paul. "There's nothin' here 'cept our kinfolk, and I promise we'll come back and visit when we're able. We're gonna be farming again!"

But Paul didn't care about the farming part. "What kind of huntin' and fishin', Pa?"

"Moose, caribou, and fish like you wouldn't believe!" His eyes lit up. "And there's trappin' in the winter, just like in that picture there with the furs. Always wanted to try some trappin'." Pa scratched his chin and grinned as he thought about it all.

"Boy, that'd be great!" Paul tried to picture life in Alaska, too. He didn't seem to notice Ma blow her nose again.

Gramps and Gran sat off to the side, listening to Pa. They, too, had sad expressions on their faces, but neither said anything.

"Minnesotans aren't the only folks going," Pa continued. "Two weeks after we leave, some families from Michigan and Wisconsin will be followin' us. Two hundred and two families all together."

"How are we gettin' there, Pa?" Minnie broke the silence.

"Well, little missy, the lady said we'd be goin' by train and ship," answered Pa, grinning. "It'll only take a couple of weeks or so." He glanced at Ma who by now had her face buried in her hands, crying harder.

"Yeah!" yelled the girls as they ran around the dining room table and up the stairs. "We're going to Alaska, we're going to Alaska!" though they hadn't the slightest idea where that was.

Paul tried to think through the details of moving. He looked over at Ma.

When Ma said it was far away she wasn't kidding! Obviously she's not as excited about this as Pa, Paul realized. *And what about all the animals, and Rascal?*

"When are we going?" Paul asked.

"Two weeks," answered Pa.

"We can take Rascal, can't we Pa?"

"I already thought about it, and I'm afraid not, son. We can take only so much. There's just no room for a dog on a long trip like that."

"But, Pa, can't we just …"

"Now Paul, I said no. I have a lot of other things to figure out before we leave."

Paul left the table and went outside. He knew he shouldn't, but he purposely let the screen door slam behind him. Rascal waited at the door with her tail wagging, looking up at him. He was crushed to think of leaving her behind. With mixed emotions, he went out to Gramps' barn to think things through about this whole move to Alaska.

"This whole thing is unbelievable and exciting—boy, what an adventure!" he said out loud as he scratched her head. "But we'll have to leave Gramps and Gran. And how can I leave you?" She licked his hand. "I kinda know how Ma feels."

The next few days were a blur as Paul's family prepared to leave. Pa got rid of whatever he could that had been in their barn at the old place. No one had extra money to buy anything, so they traded. Pa exchanged the old truck and the manure pile with his neighbor, Virgil, for an ax, a crosscut saw, and a couple of hunting rifles for those huge moose. Gramps and Gran's neighbor took the animals in exchange for a wooden barrel filled with tools, snowshoes, and traps. Minnie and Clara cried as they watched Daisy and Rosy being led down the road while the little lamb ran to keep up. Paul was sad, too, as he thought about how he had cared for them.

Pa drove the kids to school one day to see their friends one last time. Though Paul was excited about what lay ahead, he was sad to say goodbye to friends he'd grown up with. Minnie cried all the way back to her grandparents' house.

While the others were away, Gran led Ma into the living room.

"Mary, I want you to take this piano if you have room," said Gran, taking pictures and knickknacks off the top. "I know how much you loved yours, and, well you'll probably need music up there on those long winter nights."

"Are you sure, Mother?" Ma asked. "This piano's been in our family for a long time."

"I know, that's why I want you to have it," smiled Gran. "Besides, I don't ever play it anymore. It just sits here collectin' dust! It'll be my goodbye present."

"Oh, Mother!" Ma gave Gran a big hug. They both had tears running down their cheeks.

The day before their belongings were to be picked up Ma was frantically trying to pack.

"Henry! Come in here!" Ma suddenly yelled from the living room. Pa sighed as he walked toward the house.

"How in the world are we going to survive with just two thousand pounds!" Ma stood, exasperated, with her hands on her hips. Neighbors and friends had donated extra clothing and household goods after the fire, and Gran had given her pictures and sentimental items, all of which sat in piles alongside the big, upright piano in the middle of the living room.

"Well, if we didn't have to take that durned piano we'd be doin' alright," said Pa, just as exasperated. "That probably takes up half our allotment! I've got lots of tools and things, you know."

"Well I ain't leavin' this piano behind. It's from Gran, and like she said, we're gonna need some music up there to keep us sane!" said Ma. She stood thinking for a moment. "I know what I'll do," she chuckled, as she wrapped children's clothes around family pictures and packed them in the back of the piano.

Ma seems better, though I know she still ain't all that happy about movin', thought Paul as he stood in the doorway. *At least she don't cry as much. In some ways she's as stubborn as Pa. She knows just what she wants and no one's gonna change her mind.*

Her big, cast-iron frying pan was the only thing that had survived the fire. Ma put it in with the luggage they'd be carrying by train and ship all the way to Alaska, though Pa made fun of her.

"As long as I have my fryin' pan we can survive, and who knows when our other things might get there!"

"Ma, what about Rascal?" Paul asked the day before they were to leave. He'd been afraid to bring it up. The dog hadn't left his side for days, knowing that something different was in the air.

"Oh my goodness, I've been too busy to figure out what to do with her," said Ma. "Better go ask your Pa. He's in the barn." Paul didn't notice her sad face watch him as he went out the door.

"Gramps and Gran are gonna keep Rascal," Pa announced matter-of-factly as he loaded tools into a barrel. "That's the way it has to be," Pa looked at Paul. "Sorry, son. Now I've got a lot to do 'afore morning."

Paul's eyes burned and his throat felt red hot with anger and disappointment. He had secretly hoped Pa would change his mind. He turned and walked silently out of the barn.

Don't you know how much Rascal means to me? I can't go without her!

He walked along the back lane to the fields, pounding the ground with hard, angry steps. Rascal trotted beside him. When no one could see, the tears fell like rain. Man or not, he couldn't hold them in any longer. The fire, moving, and now Rascal!

The family was eating dinner when Paul returned. He sat down quietly, but didn't have an appetite. Minnie and Clara jabbered away about what Alaska would be like. Paul just moved his food around on his plate. He couldn't look at Pa.

"Aren't you hungry, Paul?" said Ma.

"Not really."

She and Gran got up to clear the table. Ma called the girls to help in the kitchen, and Gramps got the hint, too. It was obvious she wanted to leave Pa and Paul alone.

"I've had to make some hard decisions, Paul," said Pa after a while. "I'm sorry."

Pa never says he's sorry. He looked up at Pa.

"I'm sorry, too," he said quietly.

"Well, I've got to get back out to the barn." He patted Paul's shoulder as if he understood.

I still think we could find a way to take her.

Paul sighed. When Pa made up his mind it was made up—period.

Cameras clicked at the final family reunion with cousins, aunts, and uncles at Gramps' and Gran's house. Everyone hugged each other a hundred times. The women cried and waved as everyone drove away. Ma sobbed. Tears ran down Minnie's and Clara's cheeks. Paul wanted to cry, too, but he didn't.

Until now, his parents' plans hadn't seemed real. It hit Paul that the move to Alaska was final. *Will I ever see my grandparents, Rascal, or my friends again?* He felt a heavy weight in his stomach.

The flatbed truck from the county pulled up bright and early the next morning. Two men loaded their belongings, including the big piano, though not without a few profanities under their breath.

The family gave one last hug to Gramps and Gran. Paul knelt down to say goodbye to Rascal. "I'm gonna miss you terribly, girl. You take good care of Gramps and Gran now," he said affectionately as he scratched her behind the ears. She seemed to understand, and lay down next to his grandparents on the porch, her head on her paws. Paul fought back the tears.

"It's a little easier not havin' our own home," muttered Pa as they walked toward the truck.

"But this is my home and my family." Ma's eyes started to water again as she looked around at the little farm. "Let's go, before I change my mind!"

Everyone climbed into the truck. It backed slowly down the driveway and out onto the road as it made its way toward the train station. A cloud of dust rolled behind them like a thick curtain. Paul looked back one last time to see the little farm grow smaller in the distance and finally disappear altogether. *It was home,* he thought. The curtain closed.

Chapter 3
The Alaska Special

Paul, Minnie, and Clara stood quietly on the railroad platform with the crowd. They each wore their new clothes and boots from the county officials. Paul felt proud. He thought his black leather jacket was the greatest thing he had ever gotten, even at Christmas. As the big train roared to a stop, its brakes squealed and steam enveloped the cars. Shivers ran up and down Paul's spine. Excitement filled the air. Families had already traveled by smaller trains from several counties around Minnesota. Now, all waited to board the big train for their trip across America.

April 6, 1935. Paul would never forget it. When they had arrived in St. Paul, Minnesota newsmen were everywhere. Cameras flashed while bands played. Signs wished the "Alaska Colonists" a great new life in the new frontier. The mayor gave a speech about brave men and women leaving families to start a new life thousands of miles away as part of President Roosevelt's "New Deal." Cheers went up from curious crowds that gathered.

The big long train finally opened its doors. Immediately there was a rush of people with piles of luggage and pets. Lots of pets: cats, dogs, birds, and even goats. Paul couldn't believe all the animals, and thought about Rascal, but only for a moment. There was too much excitement and commotion as two hundred eighty seven fathers, mothers, and children boarded the cars and tried not to lose each other.

The whistle blew and the wheels of the train jerked forward. Children pressed their faces against the windows as they watched the crowd wave goodbye. Some mothers cried, others smiled and waved back. At first enthusiasm filled the railroad cars, but once they left the station Paul noticed how everyone became strangely silent.

Are they thinking about what's ahead, and wonderin' what their new life is really gonna be like in Alaska? Guess there's no turnin' back now!

A baby's cry broke the silence. Children chattered and conversations started up again. Paul recognized another boy his age from the first train in the seat behind him. When the boy motioned for him to join him and Ma nodded yes, Paul quickly got up and changed seats.

"Hi, my name's Erik," the boy said with a big grin. His red hair and freckles reminded Paul of his best friend back home.

"I'm Paul," he smiled. "Like your jacket." He pointed to Erik's identical leather jacket and they both laughed.

"Wanna play cards?" Erik asked.

"Sure!"

He liked Erik right away, and they spent the next several days passing the time as the "Alaska Special" wound its way first along empty fields, then through cornfields, and finally past the Rocky Mountains toward the west coast.

As the train neared the Rockies, Paul thought they were the most beautiful things he had ever seen.

"Aren't these mountains something?" he turned to Erik as they stared out the window. "I could just get off right here and not even go to Alaska."

"But I hear there are more mountains in Alaska, and way bigger!"

"I don't know how they could be any prettier," muttered Paul, half to himself. He felt sad to see them slowly vanish as they neared the coast.

"Come on, let's go eat," called Erik, "I'm starving! At least there's lots of food on this train. I aint seen so much food in my life!"

"And real fruit!" exclaimed Paul. "I'm starvin' too, now that you mention it."

The train stopped once a day for an hour. It was precious time to get up and stretch, and pure joy for the kids to run and play. The animals got to take care of business, too, while moms washed dirty diapers in the station restrooms. A common sight was diapers hanging up to dry along the windows as the westbound train snaked its way across America.

If days were tolerable, nights on the train were miserable. Seats were lowered and Paul and his sisters slept across them with legs and arms sticking out every which way.

"Move over!" Minnie ordered Clara as darkness fell and they tried to find a comfortable way to sleep.

"No, you move over!" Clara whispered loudly. She gave her sister's legs a firm kick.

"Girls!" said Ma. "Stop fussin' and go to sleep!"

Their parents slept in a semisitting position as best they could. Paul had a hard time sleeping with men snoring, especially Pa. He would stare at the diapers silhouetted against the dark sky. As they swayed in rhythm to the motion of the train they would finally lull Paul to sleep. *Strange to be hypnotized by diapers!* he thought one night just before he dozed off.

"Come, quick!" said a voice nearby early one morning.

Paul sat up and wiped the sleep from his eyes as he listened to a boy from a few seats over telling his brother some exciting news.

"You won't believe it! Ginger just had puppies! Come on!"

Several sleepy kids stumbled along behind the boy as he led them through to the storage car.

"Look!" he pointed, grinning from ear to ear.

There lay the boy's dog with five little puppies nursing peacefully. The dog looked a lot like Rascal and Paul felt a twinge of sadness when he thought about her.

"You wanna hold one?" The boy lifted a puppy up for Paul.

"We could've brought Rascal," Paul whispered as the puppy snuggled in his arms. He didn't notice Minnie watching him. She ran back and told Ma about the puppies.

Three days later the colonists arrived in San Francisco, California. It was even more amazing than St. Paul. Thousands of people turned out to cheer for the hardy people from Minnesota with more speeches and banners. A band played "Happy Days Are Here Again" while free tickets were handed out to ride trolley cars and see real movies in a theater. No one had ever done that before! They ate fancy meals, and found baskets of flowers, fruit, and candy in their hotel room every night.

"I could get used to this!" laughed Ma, who seemed to enjoy her stay in the city.

Two days later the low deep horn of the big ship that would take them to Alaska, the St. Mihiel, signaled that it was time to leave the San Francisco dock. Its departure didn't have the usual military crew on board. Instead, the horn announced the next leg of a fantastic journey of pioneers on their historic trek north. Newsmen were everywhere to record the event.

"You gotta be careful not to run into someone with a camera every time you turn around!" said Erik.

"I know! They're either asking questions or taking movies. Kind of gettin' old," agreed Paul.

After the last of the building supplies and personal belongings were finally lifted on board, the ship pulled away from the dock. Paul stood with his family on the top deck watching the thousands of well-wishers wave goodbye. He, his sisters, and Erik nibbled on cookies that a lady had handed them as they boarded.

"The people here have been so nice even though we are strangers," said Ma to Pa as they waved back. "If we don't make it in Alaska, maybe we can move back to San Francisco."

"Don't make it!" said Pa sternly. "What in the world are you talking about? Of course, we're gonna make it!"

Ma looked hurt and didn't say anything more.

"Do you think some families might go back home, Pa?" Paul was a little afraid to ask. The thought had never entered his mind that they might not stay in Alaska.

"Yes, son, I do. It's going to be a hard road ahead. Not everyone on this trip will be able to handle the tough times." His voice was strong and his face serious as he looked out to sea.

Pa turned and gave Paul a hard pat on the back. "But we're not gonna be one of 'em. Right? We're in this all the way, no matter what!"

Paul felt that heavy weight in the bottom of his stomach for the first time since they'd left home.

Just what does Pa mean by "tough times"? And what if Ma hates it up there? He looked over at Ma, who was trying to hold back more tears as she watched San Francisco's skyline fading on the horizon. *Poor Ma. Things would be so much better if she were happier.* Paul took a deep, shaky breath of the ocean breeze.

"Hey, Paul!" called Erik. "Let's do some explorin'—this ship is huge! And some fellas want us to join 'em for a game of marbles."

"Comin'!" said Paul, glad for the interruption. He took one last look at land and headed toward the bow of the ship with Erik.

"Can't wait to check this ship out! Now where is my favorite shooter?" he mumbled as he dug in his pocket. "I'm gonna win me some marbles!"

Chapter 4
Sea Sick!

"Uggggh!" moaned Ma, as she rolled over in her little wooden bunk and threw up in a bucket on the floor. The ship heaved and rolled as it headed through the open waters of the Pacific Ocean toward the Gulf of Alaska.

"Here, Ma," said Paul as he set a tray down by her bunk. "How are Minnie and Clara doin'?"

"Check on 'em, would ya, Paul?" Ma said weakly. "I can't even raise my head without gettin' sick."

Paul bent over another wooden bunk that the girls shared. Their pale faces looked up at him. The smell of vomit was so strong Paul had to pinch his nose to keep from gagging.

"You're not supposed to be on this side of the ship," said Minnie in a faint little voice. "This side is for ladies only."

Paul smiled. "Well, I guess you can't be too sick if you're bossing me around!" He helped each of them take a few sips of tea and left some crackers to nibble on. "I'll be back to check on you in a little while."

"Thanks, dear. I'm glad you're not seasick, too," Ma smiled. "How's Pa doin'?"

"Oh, he's bein' interviewed by one of those reporters right now. Said he'd come down in a while to check on all his girls."

Paul made his way up the steps to the deck to meet Erik as fast as he could and took several deep breaths of the ocean air. "Whew! I can't get that smell out of my nose!"

"How're they doin'?" asked Erik, who was busy counting marbles from his bulging pockets.

"Not too good. The whole place is full of women and kids moanin' and throwin' up!"

"Ugh! Glad I'm not sick. Hey, look at this cat's eye!" Erik seemed more interested in his marbles.

"Yeah, that's a pretty one."

"Wanna see if we can find more? They're rollin' all over the ship. Finders keepers!"

Erik's silly grin always made Paul laugh. "Sure."

"Did you see that reporter asking your Pa questions? They actually had a movie camera on him!"

"Yeah, he seemed to like it, too! Good thing they didn't ask Ma what she thought about the whole thing so far!"

The boys laughed as they searched for marbles along the deck, grabbing the rails and walking as if they were drunk while the ship lunged and rolled.

"Look, there's one!" Erik spotted a marble in a crack of the deck and went to reach for it.

Just then the ship leaned and the marble rolled over the side and into the water.

"Dang!" sighed Erik as he looked down into the water.

"Forget the marble! Would ya look at that?" Paul pointed to something in the water off the ship's bow.

"Holy smokes!" exclaimed Erik. "Whales!"

A small crowd of people made their way to the front of the ship. "Them are humpbacks," said one of the crewmen, as he spit tobacco over the rail. "They winter in California and head back to Alaska in the summer."

One whale jumped completely out of the water and landed with a splash. "That there's called breachin'," the crewman grinned, revealing several missing teeth. "Guess they're escortin' us north!"

Paul and Erik watched in fascination as the whales' backs and tails dipped and rose gracefully out of the water. Finally, they disappeared on the horizon.

"Just think," said Paul. "Everyone back in Minnesota is in school right this minute while we stand on the bow of a ship watchin' whales breach on our way to Alaska!" They both laughed and whooped with joy.

A few days later the engines of the St. Mihiel finally slowed as it made its way around a huge rock island and into Seward's harbor. The big ship slid past sea lions sunning themselves on the rocks, and sea otters floating beside the ship on their backs. Their silly expressions made the passengers laugh.

Calm waters of Resurrection Bay spread before them like gray slate. Magnificent, snow-capped mountains surrounded the bay, their peaks partially hidden behind low layers of clouds. All the colonists made their way to the deck, even those who had been sick, for their first sight of Alaska. Men, women, and children stood quietly to take in the magnitude of their new home, undaunted by the cool, gray greeting.

"Look at that glacier!" Paul whispered as he pointed, not wanting to spoil the moment. "It comes right down into the bay!"

"Wow!" answered Erik, speechless for once.

Perhaps the captain was mesmerized too, because as they neared the dock, wood suddenly splintered and buckled as the ship came in too fast and smashed into it. A few passengers screamed. Dock workers scrambled to bring the huge ship under control and lash her down.

Everyone was more than anxious to get off the ship, though they were soon disappointed. "I'm sorry folks, but you're not going to be able to leave just yet," the captain announced to those gathered near him. "Since the transient workers are getting a late start, you're going to have to stay on board for a few more days till they can get your tents set up."

"Ma," Clara tugged on Ma's skirt as she stood there speechless. "What are transient workers?"

"They're the workers hired to put up our tents and help build our houses and barns and whatever else needs to be done," answered Pa. "Most came from California on another ship and a few rode with us, but the other ship was delayed and just arrived yesterday. See it over there?" He pointed to a ship docked near theirs. "They still need to get all those things unloaded and up to the Matanuska

Valley for us 'afore we get there. Looks like it might be a while yet," Pa chuckled.

Despite Pa's positive attitude, many of the colonists were shocked and unhappy, especially Ma. She started crying while Minnie and Clara clung weakly to her skirt.

"I don't think I can stand it!" She plopped down on a barrel on the deck, put her face in her hands, and wept.

"Course you can!" said Pa, impatiently. "There's nothin' we can do about it so might as well make the best of it. Try to pull yourself together, Mary!"

After much moaning and complaining by more than a few folks, the crew finally let people off the ship, but only under certain conditions.

"There have been some cases of measles on board, so you're not to go into town. You can walk along the shore if you want. When you hear the bell, it's time to return."

"Come on!" urged Paul. He and Erik couldn't wait to go exploring. They were even more than happy to take Minnie and Clara, who were feeling much better.

"Is the ground rolling? It feels like we're still on the ship!" giggled Minnie as they walked along the dock.

They all laughed when they tried to walk straight though their legs wobbled.

"I can't wait to check out the ocean," said Erik. "There sure aren't any of these in Minnesota!"

Several hours were spent beachcombing. They watched sea otters dip and float a few feet offshore, using small rocks to break clams and mussels open on their tummies. The girls gathered pockets full of shells to take back to Ma. Little tide pools along the beach held star fish, anemones, and other sea creatures they'd never seen before.

The bell rang. When they finally boarded the ship for dinner, Pa took Paul aside.

"A bunch of fellas are going fishin' in the morning. Wanna go?" Pa had a twinkle in his eye that Paul hadn't seen in a long time.

Pa actually wants to do something fun? Wow, we're goin' fishing! Paul was so excited he hardly slept that night in his little bunk.

After breakfast the next day, Pa managed to round up a couple of poles and the two headed along the shore to fish away from the others.

"I thought you wanted to fish with some of the other men?" said Paul.

"Well, two solid weeks with the same people is a long time. Thought we'd get away from all the folks for a bit." He showed Paul how to bait his hook with some small pieces of fish the cook had given the fishermen that morning.

"It's like paradise fishin' here in the ocean with this scenery and all," Pa sighed. "When they said Alaska was cold and barren I sure didn't picture this, did you?"

"Nope!"

"This country is already in my blood, Paul, and we ain't even been here a week!"

"I kinda feel that way, too." Paul smiled at Pa.

"Paul, I got a surprise for ya," Pa said nonchalantly after a while, as he cast his line into the water.

"Yeah?" Paul didn't know if life could get any better than this.

"I know how much yer missin' Rascal. I've felt bad we didn't bring her now that I see how many brought animals."

Paul froze and stared at Pa to hear more.

Pa laughed. "Minnie mentioned the puppies on the train, and I asked the boy who owns Ginger if you could have one. Would ya like that?"

"Would I!" Paul nearly dropped his pole.

"Well, you'll have to take care of her and make her behave."

"Oh, I can do that!"

"And they're only a couple of weeks old so they won't be weaned for another month. Can you wait—?"

Just then Pa's pole bent hard as a fish bit the hook. It took all his concentration to bring the big salmon in, but it got loose just as Pa was going to grab it.

While he hoped for a fish to bite his line, too, Paul happily thought about having a dog again.

It wasn't long before Paul felt his line go taut, and for the next twenty minutes he forgot about the dog as he pulled and reeled in a big fish, fresh from the sea. This one didn't get away.

Neither said much more, but never was there a prouder father or son as when they placed the fish in the cook's tub.

As they headed back up the gangplank, Pa smiled and put his hand on Paul's shoulder. "Even though I lost a big one, that was the most fun I've had since I was a kid like you!"

Paul's face beamed with happiness. "That was the most fun I've had since I was a kid like me, too!" He didn't care if men weren't supposed to show emotion. He had never been happier in his whole life and he was already hooked on Alaska!

Chapter 5
Home Away From Home

After three days in Seward, the colonists were elated to finally disembark from the ship and board the train to Anchorage.

"There you are!" said a voice. "Where've you been?"

Paul jumped. He sat looking out the train window as it made its way around and through mountains toward Anchorage, his puppy asleep in his lap. Unless it was feeding time, little Belle was rarely out of Paul's sight.

"I've been right here. Where've you been?"

"Playin' rummy with some kids in the next car," said Erik. "One kid started cheatin' so I quit."

Paul laughed. "Can you believe all this?" he gestured at the view.

"Told you there were more mountains up here!" replied Erik. "Wasn't comin' outta that last tunnel something? I thought we might roll right off the track and down into that gorge!"

The railroad car rocked gently from side to side as it snaked its way around huge mountains, past waterfalls gushing with melting snow, and through wide valleys dotted with spruce and birch trees ready to pop open with the green of new life.

Belle suddenly woke up and climbed up onto Erik to lick his face, her little tail wagging gleefully.

"Hey you, Belle-Belle. That tickles. Ouch! Don't bite, little gal." Erik loved playing with Belle.

But Paul seemed quiet and pensive. "You excited about moving up here?" he asked Erik.

Erik nodded. "You bet! My pa's from Finland and his parents brought him to Minnesota when he was twelve. So, I guess it's natural that I'm movin' so far away. If my parents weren't both so excited about all this, it might be different." He studied Paul's face for a moment. "What about you?'

Paul shrugged his shoulders. "Oh, just wish my ma were more excited about it instead of crying ever since we left. Bein' seasick on the boat didn't help!" Both boys laughed. "When they said we'd have to spend three more nights on board so the workers could get tents set up, I thought she might start walking back to Minnesota!" They laughed harder.

Suddenly the train slowed and groaned as it descended and curved sharply.

"Wow, look at that! We're actually going under the back part of the train!" Erik exclaimed as they craned their necks to see out the window. Sure enough, the descent was so steep that the train actually looked like a roller coaster, doubling back on itself. The conductor walked through the cars, proudly explaining the event.

"We're fifty miles from Seward, folks, and this is what we call 'the Loop,'" he said. "The track makes a complete loop, crossing over itself. There are three miles of track to go a half mile as the crow flies in order to descend into the Placer River Valley. It's quite a sight, isn't it?" The conductor chuckled and left to visit the next car with the same speech.

"Kinda makes my stomach flip-flop," said Erik, looking queasy.

"Wow," was all Paul could say as he studied the miles of wooden trestle that held the train track in place. "How can it hold us up? Sure hope it's not rotten anywhere!"

"That's reassuring!" Erik sat back in his seat. "Don't think I want to see it right now."

"Hey, you do look a little pale!" Paul jabbed him in the ribs.

"Naw, I'm fine. See there, I think we're at the bottom." Erik smiled weakly.

A few minutes later the train entered another tunnel and the rhythmic sound of the wheels clanged loudly. The boys were silent until it came out the other end.

"Wonder how hard it'll be to farm up here. Heard one man say it hadn't been done with much success before this."

"Aw, you worry too much! It probably won't be much different than doin' chores back home. Besides, we can help each other, right?" Erik gave Paul a slug in the arm.

"Yeah? How much work do you ever do? Let me see your muscles." Paul pushed his sleeve up and tightened his biceps. "Bet I can beat you at arm wrestling!"

"Gosh, you are pretty strong," admitted Erik when Paul easily beat him. "I have a strange feelin' you don't like to lose, either!"

"Not if I can help it!"

Farther along the train entered yet another tunnel. This one opened up to a huge lake, surrounded by majestic, jagged mountains. Passengers oohed and aahed at the beautiful turquoise color of the water as the train wound around its shore. Someone from the next seat mentioned the color was from glaciers that fed into the lake.

What a different world from Minnesota! Paul marveled at it all.

More tunnels, gorges, and an occasional moose kept the boys busy for the rest of the trip. Houses and buildings of Anchorage came into view, and the train slowed to a stop at the station. Paul took Belle back to her mother and she eagerly settled in for a snack.

The weary colonists disembarked, were herded into all the cars Anchorage residents could round up, and taken to the Community Center for a feast prepared by their new fellow Alaskans.

"What's this?" Paul pointed to a plate heaped with dark meat as they all sat at long tables with dishes of strange-looking food.

"That's black bear meat, that over there is moose, and this is smoked salmon," said a friendly woman, making sure the platters stayed heaped with food.

"Well, pass it over here, please!" Paul exclaimed. Someday I'm going to get me a moose!" He was eager to try it all, and seemed to forget his worries for the time being.

Three hours later the train rounded the final bend and crossed the

Knik and Matanuska rivers. The mountains opened into a broad valley. Gray, gloomy skies were spitting rain.

"Ladies and gentlemen, your final stop is ahead!" announced Colonel Olson, manager of the Alaska Railroad, as he came through the cars. "Today is the tenth of May, and your long journey is over. Welcome to Matanuska Valley and best wishes to each of you as you start your new life!"

Cheers and applause rang out in car after car as the colonists peered out the windows and stood at the half doors between cars to get a better look. Paul noticed that on one side of the train rows and rows of new white canvas tents stood in a clearing near the station. A few curious homesteaders and miners stood around to watch the newcomers. After fifteen days of travel, the colonists were so eager to get off the train and find their new home in tent city they didn't care what the Matanuska Valley looked like.

Well, most didn't care.

"Oh, great," moaned Ma when she stepped off the train steps in her dress and heels, and sank six inches in mud. "We've come all this way to mud, rain, and—what was that?" she said as she swatted at something buzzing around her face. "Look at 'em all!"

The girls started to swat their arms and ran around Ma's skirt to try to get away from the swarming insects.

"Did I forget to tell you about the mosquitoes, Mary?" said Pa. "You'll get used to 'em after a while. Come on, let's go ask someone which of these dozens of tents is ours."

"Erik," whispered Paul as they were parting. "Meet me at that water pump over there after you're all settled, okay?"

"Got it! Bye!" said Erik as he slapped a mosquito on his forehead and ran to catch up to his family.

It was chaos as families, luggage, and animals were unloaded from the train. By the time the new Alaskans had figured out who had which tent and settled in, everyone was exhausted and hungry.

"Well, here's our new home for a while!" announced Pa as he pulled back the tent flaps and the weary family stood looking inside. "All fourteen by twenty feet of it."

"Cots, a table, a bucket, and a stove," sighed Ma. "Not exactly a luxury hotel. At least there's a wooden floor to get away from this mud!"

"Well, I'm hungry and time's a-wastin'," said Pa. "I see there's a pile of coal here by the tent. I'll get the stove fired up and figure out where to get some food."

"Hullo!" came a friendly voice from the next tent over. "I'm Margaret. You don't happen to know where we can get any cooking utensils by any chance?"

"As a matter of fact, I do!" Ma smiled for the first time in a long time. She opened one of the canvas bags and rummaged around. "I thought this might come in handy!" She gave Pa an "I told you so" look as she held up the big frying pan.

"Do ya mind if we join you for some grub this evening?" asked Margaret's husband.

"By all means!" Ma suddenly seemed happy to be having company.

"Paul, can you find water?" said Pa. "I'll go find the commissary."

Erik was waiting at the pump and waved to Paul when he saw him in the distance. "What tent you in?"

"Number seventy-four. How 'bout you?"

"Fifty-three, a couple a rows away." Erik pointed. "This is something, ain't it? All these tents up. This is gonna to be fun!"

Paul, always more practical than Erik, was watching for water to flow into the bucket after raising and lowering the squeaky handle a dozen times. "Lots of fun. And I have a feeling there's gonna be lots of haulin' water, too."

"Well, maybe, but this place is great! I feel at home already." Erik spread his arms out and breathed in the cool, clean air. "Can't wait to do some explorin'!"

"Yeah, me either." Paul looked around at the mountains that surrounded the flat, wooded valley. "Sure are lots a trees around here. Pretty hard to believe this land is supposed to be cleared and ready to farm by the end of the summer."

"Well, first things first!" Erik laughed. "I'm gettin' hungry even after all that Alaskan food."

"What's your family doin' for supper?"

"They're trying to figure that out. They're servin' food in one of the rail cars, but my ma won't step foot on a train for a long time if she can help it!" Erik laughed.

"Come on over to our tent. Ma has the only frying pan around and Pa went to get food at the commissary."

Paul trudged back to the tent in the mud while Erik went to tell his family about dinner. By the time everyone had gathered, Pa had a fire glowing in the cookstove. He served camp coffee while Ma and Margaret made bacon, eggs, canned beans, and bread with butter.

"I declare, Mary," Pa said. "I think this is the most delicious supper I've ever had! Here's a toast to our new home! We're not Minnesotans anymore. We're Alaskans!" He raised his coffee cup and everyone else did the same with much cheering.

I don't think I've ever seen Pa so happy. He loves this whole thing!

For several hours the families laughed and recalled stories about their adventures en route to the Matanuska Valley. The nighttime sky hardly darkened, and it was late before Ma realized she hadn't seen Minnie and Clara for a while.

"Land sakes, where are the girls?" her voice was full of worry.

"Right here, Ma," whispered Paul. Minnie and Clara were snuggled together on a cot, sandwiched between travel bags like two little kittens, sound asleep. It had been a long trip!

Everyone laughed and decided they were ready to do the same thing. Good nights were said and laughter could be heard all around the tent city as folks headed to bed.

I miss Gramps and Gran, but this is like a big new family, thought Paul.

"Ugh, hope we don't have to sleep on these cots for too long. They're awful!" groaned Ma as she tried to get comfortable. But before two minutes had passed you could hear her snoring.

Everyone slept like a log that first night.

Chapter 6
The Lottery

Though ten thirty at night, the sun still shone as Pa stood in the doorway of their tent smoking his pipe.

"Look at all them kids," he muttered half to himself and half to Ma. "Dozens of 'em, all screamin' and playin' like they was in heaven!"

Kids of all ages ran through the rows of tents laughing and yelling. They chased barking dogs and played kick the can, tag, and ante over. Older kids played baseball all day and into the evening.

"I've never seen such a pitiful bunch of kids covered in mud and dirt and full of mosquito bites," he chuckled between puffs. "Listen to 'em laugh. They're havin' the time of their life."

Ma smiled but didn't answer as she scrubbed clothes by hand on the washboard.

"No one's any different here—not richer or poorer—than anyone else," he continued. "It don't matter if they have shoes, or holes in their clothes. They all came from the same situation and all live in tents like everyone else. Think how much better it'd be if nobody judged anyone else like that."

"Yeah, I reckon you're right," Ma muttered.

There was a long silence as she poured hot water into another tub for rinsing.

"Them folks from Michigan and Wisconsin are supposed to arrive tomorrow," he said. "There'll be nearly a thousand men, women and kids by the time we're all together—imagine that. Glad I'm not organizing this operation!" He shook his head. "I don't see where they're gonna put 'em. The transient workers don't have near enough tents put up for another hundred thirty six families."

"They'll come up with something," said Ma as she dumped the wash water out the door. Wet clothes hung over ropes strung inside and outside the tent. "Nothin's gone as planned yet, and I don't expect it to change much."

"Here," she handed Pa a bucket. "Do you mind fetchin' some water from the pump? And see if you can round up those kids. It's nearly midnight and they need to get to bed!"

The next day was the most important day yet. As soon as the Michigan and Wisconsin men arrived from Seward, a drawing was to be held to determine where families would live. That afternoon everyone stood around the tracks waiting for the train to pull up.

"I hear it's just the men on the train. The womenfolk and kids had to stay on the boat," whispered Erik to Paul as they stood near their families and watched with curiosity. Belle sat at Paul's feet with a cord for a leash held in his hand.

"Yeah, that's what I heard, too," nodded Paul. "Bunch of kids have measles. Look, here it comes." He pointed down the tracks.

A puff of smoke appeared as the train slowly wound around the last bend. It blew its whistle and squealed to a stop in front of the railroad car that served as the station.

"There's Colonel Olson with Mr. Irwin," Paul tipped his head toward the two men standing on the platform. Belle barked at the train. "Shhh, Belle. This is very important business. You better be quiet," he said patiently. She sat down, but whined softly.

"Yeah, Olson runs the whole railroad," whispered Erik. "And Mr. Irwin is supposed to figure out how to keep everyone happy here and in Washington D.C. My pa says it'll be a pretty tough job. He says President Roosevelt and his New Deal ideas to put people to work might look good on paper, but making them happen with two hundred two real families is not going to be easy."

"You mean we're all kind of an experiment?" asked Paul.

"I suppose you could put it that way." Erik shrugged.

Men and older teenagers disembarked from the train. They hadn't been treated to an Alaskan meal in Anchorage like the Minnesotans, and looked tired and worn.

"You gonna stay for the drawing?" asked Erik.

"Course! I can't wait to see if we're gonna live near each other." Paul gave Erik a friendly elbow to the ribs.

Mr. Irwin had climbed up on a platform while the men gathered around. Women and children stood quietly or found wooden boxes to sit on while they held their babies and their breaths to see where their new home would be. It was a bright, sunny day. Everyone squinted or held their hands up over their eyes to watch and listen to Mr. Irwin give directions.

"Now this is the way we're going to do this," he announced. "First, we'll draw a number for who goes in what order. Then we'll draw again for the forty- or eighty-acre parcel you'll call home. Any questions?"

"Yeah," called out one man. "What if we don't like the parcel we get?"

"If you can find someone to trade with, that's fine. You've got a month to switch. Otherwise, you're out of luck. Okay, let's get started. Suzanne, where's the box of numbers?"

"Right here, sir, ready to go," a pretty young lady replied as she stood nearby with what looked like a shoebox.

Mr. Irwin and Colonel Olson both smiled broadly as one by one the men drew the first number. They had spent many hours, days, and months planning for this moment. As the tracts of land were drawn, each man ran over to a big map posted on a wooden board to see where their new home would be located.

"Henry Jacobs, number one hundred thirty seven," called Pa as he drew his number. He came back from the board with a smile on his face.

"I like the area," he said with a relieved voice. "Paul, let's go check it out first thing in the morning."

Paul nodded with a smile, too.

Erik's family drew a parcel about a half mile away from Paul's. The boys couldn't contain their excitement about being so close together. They laughed while they pushed and hit each other playfully. Belle sensed their happiness and jumped up and down.

The families in Paul's and Erik's area would move their tents to make a smaller tent city, called Camp 8. Eventually, when enough land was cleared, they would move their tents to their own home-sites. For now there would be ten smaller camps in all.

When the drawing was over, most men seemed happy with their parcels, though a few were already complaining.

The same people seem to complain about everything, noticed Paul. *Wonder if they'll be the first ones to go back.*

"Come on, let's play ball!" yelled some kids as they sprinted toward the open field.

"Race ya," teased Erik.

They both took off for the field, with Belle trailing behind.

Chapter 7
Maggie

Three days later the train pulled into the station with the Michigan and Wisconsin women and children. Though they were treated to an Alaskan lunch in Anchorage, they were exhausted, especially the mothers with babies and little ones.

One woman was nearly hysterical as she looked out the window for her husband while trying to keep her young children from fighting.

"Where is my Walter? Heavens, I'll never find him with all these people!" she cried.

A pretty lady patted the woman's arm to console her, all the while searching the crowd for her own husband. Her daughter, Maggie, couldn't remember when her mother had ever looked so tired.

People hurried here and there, trying to find their families and making their way toward tent city. Horses stomped their feet impatiently, men shouted directions, and mothers yelled for their children to stay near them. Curious Minnesotans stood watching the commotion, while Michigan and Wisconsin husbands tried to find their families.

"Helen," a man's voice was heard through the noise. "Over here!"

The man and an older boy pulled a horse-drawn wagon up to the train.

"William, Michael! Are we ever glad to see you!" smiled Maggie's mother. "Where in the world did you get ahold of a horse and wagon?"

"Oh, I have my connections," he winked. They loaded their belongings, including a cage of ducks. Mother, Maggie, and her brother, David, climbed up on the wagon. All were happy to be back together.

From the back of the wagon, eleven-year-old Maggie looked around at her new home. Suddenly, her father stopped the wagon.

"Hi, Henry," he said to a man along the road. "I'd like you to meet my wife, Helen, my sons, David and Michael, and my daughter, Maggie. Helen, this is Henry and his son, Paul, our new neighbors."

"Nice to meet you all," they both said, with a smile.

"David and Michael, do you want to join us for a baseball game after you're settled in?"

Paul pointed to the open field on the other side of the tents.

"Sure!" they replied, eager to get some exercise.

"Can I play, too?" came a girl's voice.

Paul noticed Maggie for the first time and smiled. "I don't see why not. Lots of girls play—if you know how."

"Oh, I know how!" she exclaimed.

"Yeah, you have to watch her," said David with a grin. "She was the best base-stealer in our whole school!"

Everyone laughed as Maggie's father slapped the reins lightly and started toward tent number sixty-five.

Maggie looked back and saw Paul standing with his thumbs hooked in the belt loops of his pants, watching them and smiling. The sun lit up his curly blond hair. He was too far away for him to notice her blush.

When they arrived at their tent, Father had a fire going, the kettle hot for a cup of tea, and the beds made. Home had never looked so good!

"We're lucky," he said. "Some of the families have to double up with folks from Minnesota until they can get enough tents up!"

After supper Maggie ran to find her friend Francine's tent, but she was busy helping her mother feed and calm tired, cranky little ones for bed. So Maggie and her brothers headed out to the baseball field, and for several hours, kids from Minnesota, Michigan, and Wisconsin played ball in the land of the midnight sun. They laughed, joked, and played like they'd been friends all their lives. A few parents finally came out to remind everyone that it was late and time for bed.

"Father," said Maggie as he tucked her into her cot. "Where's Francine's home going to be? She was too busy to talk much."

"They're going to be living in the Butte, which is pretty far away from us, I'm afraid."

"How far?"

"Oh, about ten miles, I think."

"Oh," sighed Maggie. She thought for a moment and smiled. "That's okay, she's still my best friend and we'll find ways to see each other. Isn't it funny that we both ended up coming to Alaska?"

"Yes, and I'm sure you'll find ways to visit," grinned Father.

"Do you like our new property?"

"Wait till you see it, Maggie May. You're going to love it!"

"Can we go there tomorrow?"

"Of course. I can't wait to show Mother and the boys, too. Now go to sleep. It's been a very long day."

"Yes, it has." She sighed contentedly. "I just have to write in my diary."

"Okay, good night." Father kissed her forehead and crawled into bed. Mother and her brothers were already asleep.

Maggie snuggled down in her cot with a smile on her face as she thought about what to write.

> *Dear Diary,*
>
> *We're here! I can't believe it! As soon as we got off the train in the Matanuska Valley I felt like I belonged here! Tent #65 is our home for a while until we move to Camp 8. Father says our property is beautiful. I can't wait to see it. Played ball with kids past midnight! Met a boy named Paul. Has pretty blue eyes. Well, sooo tired. Good night, new home!*
>
> *Love, Maggie*

Though a few kids were still outside yelling and playing, she never slept so soundly as that first night in the Matanuska Valley.

Chapter 8
Tent City

Maggie looked around as she stood in front of the tent door holding a crude broom fashioned from sticks and branches. After breakfast she had helped her mother wash dishes, then swept never-ending dirt out of the tent. Her brothers had gone with Father to pick up their shipped household goods from the Matanuska train station, five miles back toward Anchorage. Unless it rained, Father promised to take Maggie to see their new homesite later.

"Good mornin'," said a man from the tent next door as he sat at his grindstone, a large stone wheel he turned with a foot pedal to sharpen his ax. "Looks like rain."

"I hope not," Maggie answered cheerfully, undaunted by the weather.

Gloomy, gray skies greeted her. The wind whipped at her face. Sheets of rain were visible here and there around the great valley. The tent flaps slapped in an irritated sort of way as gusts of wind blew through. At first, Mother had run outside to pound the tent stakes deeper into the ground.

"I declare," she had said, her hair tousled as she struggled back into the tent. "It feels like we're going to take off into space!"

Maggie had laughed to see her proper mother with her hair all wind-blown.

A little girl stopped in front of the tent and looked up at Maggie. "You wanna play ante ova?" Smudges of dirt covered her face.

"Aren't you Clara under all that dirt?" asked Maggie. "Paul's little sister?"

Clara nodded, her face streaked with mud.

Maggie laughed. "Well, how do you play?"

Clara rolled her eyes in disbelief. "One kid thwows the ball ova the tent and the other kid catches it while the kid that thwowed the ball wuns awound the tent and twies not to get tagged by the one that catches the ball. Okay?" She took a deep breath and waited for some sign that Maggie understood. All Maggie could do was laugh.

A sudden gust of wind caused both girls to close their eyes and mouth tight and lower their heads until it passed through. The wind brought with it clouds of powdery silt from the nearby glacier, covering everything with fine, black dust. It got into eyes and ears and hair and teeth, in dishes and bedding and clothing.

"Well, do ya?" Clara tugged impatiently on her sleeve again.

"Not right now, Clara," said Maggie, rubbing her eyes. "I just got here yesterday, and I want to look around a little first. Maybe later, okay?"

"Okay," sighed Clara dejectedly.

Just then a scraggly dog with several puppies trailing behind ran past. Clara's face lit up.

"Hey, little Belle, wait fow me!" she giggled as she ran to catch up, joining Minnie and several other laughing, dirty kids.

Maggie smiled and poked her head back inside the tent. "Can I go look around a little, Mother? I want to see how Francine's doing and check things out."

"Be back by lunch," her mother answered. "And don't go across the tracks!"

Off she skipped. As she neared Francine's tent, she could see her little brother throw a ball over it while Francine waited to catch it. Her brother then sprinted around the tent as fast as he could, laughing uncontrollably, while Francine tried to tag him with the ball.

"Let me guess. You're playing ante over?" Maggie laughed.

"Maggie! It's so good to see you! Yes, some kids from Minnesota taught Jimmy and we've been playing it all morning. I'm so glad you stopped by so I could take a break!"

"Well, I wondered if you'd like to go exploring."

"I'd love to, but I'll have to ask Mother. The baby is due soon, you know, and she's pretty tired after the trip. Let's go inside, Jimmy. I'll get you a little snack. That's a good boy."

"You sure sound like a mother!"

"Well, if you had four little brothers and sisters you would, too!" Francine laughed. "I'll be right back." A few moments later she jumped down off the tent platform.

"Mother said it's fine as long as I'm not gone too long and we stop at the commissary for some milk."

"Sure, I haven't been there yet."

They headed toward the railroad tracks.

"Mother warned me not to go across the tracks or she'll probably have me do laundry by hand for the next month!" said Maggie.

"She knows you too well," giggled Francine.

"I'm going to be good," Maggie said in a determined voice. "Besides, it doesn't look like there's much over there except the post office."

"Those men are changing the name of the town from Wharton to Palmer. I found out George Palmer was the first settler to own a store here back in the late 1800s."

"How do you know that? We've both been here only a couple of days!"

"Our tent happens to be beside a woman from Minnesota who loves to gossip. As soon as she met Mother, she had to start in on all the goings-on around here. Says she got all the news from some homesteaders that have been here for a while, though I don't really believe everything she says."

"So what about George Palmer?"

"Well, he had a store in Knik, an area a ways from here, and built another one near here. But no one worked in this one! He just trusted the miners, homesteaders, and trappers to leave money for the things they bought."

"Do you think people were honest?"

"The story goes that no one ever stole from Mr. Palmer's store. Isn't that amazing?"

Maggie nodded. "It sure is."

"Hey, look at this!" Maggie stopped in front of a tent that had the word "Library" written on a sign on the door. "I didn't know there was a library! Let's go in."

She and Francine browsed through the few books that had been gathered and stacked on some wobbly shelves. Each borrowed a book with the promise to return it in a week or two.

"Let's head over to the commissary, okay?" Francine pointed away from the tracks and toward the water tower being built.

Supplies and equipment lay everywhere. It looked like a mountain range of tools, lumber, and miscellaneous items beside a sea of tents.

"Boo!" Suddenly someone jumped out from behind a stack of porcelain sinks. Both girls screamed and jumped.

"Paul! You scared us to death!" exclaimed Maggie.

"Ha!" laughed Paul. "Your mother said I'd probably find you over this way." He grinned and put his hands in his pockets as he walked beside her.

"This is Francine, my very best friend. Francine, this is Paul. We're going to be next-door neighbors!"

Francine smiled at Paul. "Nice to meet you."

"Hi. So, how did best friends get to come up to Alaska together?" Paul wondered.

"Oh, that was so great!" Francine answered eagerly before Maggie could take a breath. "Maggie came over one day and said, 'Francine, I have a secret and it's both good and bad.' And I said, 'I have one, too!' So I said, 'You go first,' and Maggie said, 'No, you go first!' And then when she said her family had been picked to go to Alaska I yelled, 'Mine, too!' and we hugged and yelled and danced around so that Mother thought we had gone half crazy!"

Paul looked at them both as if he agreed, partly because he had never heard anyone talk so fast and partly because of the story.

"It's amazing but true!" nodded Maggie. "But now Francine's family will be moving to the Butte, so I won't get to see her as much as I'd like." She made a sad face and hooked her arm through Francine's.

"I have a feeling you'll find a way," laughed Paul.

"What've you been up to?" Maggie looked over at him.

"Well, I just got back with Pa. We marked the trees to clear for our house. It's going to be a lot of work, but we're hoping the transient workers can get started clearing tomorrow."

"Wow, your father doesn't waste any time, does he?" said Francine.

"No, he's afraid things won't be done before winter if they don't get started soon. Somehow the workers have to clear trees and get houses built for every family here before winter hits, which I hear can be October!"

"October?" both girls said at once.

"Plus, they're working on all these?" Maggie waved her arm to include the commissary, warehouses, and water tower that were being built.

"It looks like a colony of ants, not farmers!" laughed Paul.

Men swarmed on and around piles of equipment, rode horses back and forth, and hammered on new buildings. President Roosevelt had ordered at least one hundred transient workers from California to do everything for the colonists. For two dollars a month they were to clear the land and build houses, barns, office buildings, the commissary, a church, and a school—everything a little town would need, in just a few months.

"It wouldn't have been so bad if the workers had come as planned. But something happened and most of them came on the same ship with us." said Paul. "Now everyone's supposed to just sit around and wait! Pa thinks it's crazy that people can't help build their own places. Lots of people are pretty unhappy."

"Hey, what's the big idea?" a man yelled angrily as he stood in line outside a tent up ahead. "I've got some complaints and I plan to tell Mr. Irwin all about 'em!"

Another gentleman in the line seemed to be trying to calm him down without success.

As the three approached, they noticed the sign on the tent door, "Project Manager, ARRC."

A tall, thin man came out the door after hearing the commotion.

"That's Don Irwin, head of this whole operation," whispered Paul. "ARRC stands for Alaska Rural Rehabilitation Corporation."

"What seems to be the problem here?" Mr. Irwin said in a kind, patient voice.

"I'm sick and tired of not getting the things we need," yelled the angry man. "Some of our belongings aren't here yet, and my wife thinks the prices of food at the commissary are too high, and my baby's sick, and …"

"Just a minute, sir," said Mr. Irwin, putting his hand up to try to calm him down. "There are several people in front of you that have complaints of their own. You'll just have to wait your turn and I'll be with you as soon as I can." He turned, and with his tall legs, was back through the door in two strides while the man mumbled angrily to himself.

"Come on, let's hurry past." Paul was afraid there might be a fight. "See what I mean about people getting upset about things?"

Farther ahead, they could hear two more men having a conversation. One was obviously frustrated.

"Well boss, these hundred and twenty horses came in off the train today, but there ain't no wagons. What should we do with 'em?"

"I'll go talk to Mr. Irwin right now and find out where the wagons are. You figure out where to keep the horses for a few days."

The man just given orders to care for one hundred twenty horses sighed, took his cap off and scratched his head.

"Poor Mr. Irwin," sighed Maggie. "He sure has lots of problems to solve and people to try to keep happy!"

"I wonder where those poor horses will end up," said Francine sympathetically.

They climbed the steps to the commissary and wandered amongst mounds of food and items that seemed to cover every inch of the room.

"Hmm. Five cents for a banana. It sure don't look very appealing, if you know what I mean!" teased Paul.

"Oh, you're so clever!" Maggie said sarcastically.

"Look at this. Seventy-five cents for milk. These prices sure do seem high! But, Mother said to get some." Francine shrugged her shoulders and told the clerk her father's name.

"That's all you have to do when you buy something?" said Maggie.

"Guess so," said Francine.

"Yep, they keep track of how much each family spends," said Paul. "We're supposed to keep it under a certain amount depending on the size of your family, but some folks think they can order the whole store. Pa says they'll be sorry—it's got to be paid back eventually!"

"Wow, things sure are different from back home!" said Francine. "You'd think people would be thankful to be able to buy food like this."

"You guys just got here, but you'll start to hear a lot of grumbling before too long."

"Well, I love it here!" said Maggie cheerfully as they hopped down the steps and back toward tent city. "They can complain all they want!"

"If you can't tell, Maggie's an optimist!" laughed Francine.

"Yeah, I kind of figured that," Paul smiled. "Hey, we're moving the tent out to Camp 8 in a couple of days. When are you all going?" he asked.

"We're staying here at the main camp for a while," said Francine. "They really don't have much of a road out to the Butte yet."

"And Father hasn't said," Maggie replied. "I still haven't even seen our property. We were going to go out later today, but—"

"Look out!" Francine motioned them to stop as a photographer's camera flashed a picture of a bunch of dirty ragged kids with big grins lined up on a long beam between tents. Maggie, Francine, and Paul laughed to watch them.

Suddenly, the heavy, dark clouds that had loomed ominously all day let go. Sheets of rain swirled around them, mixed with silt and dust.

"Race you back!" yelled Paul, who got a head start.

Off they ran dodging kids, dogs, mothers frantically taking laundry off clothes lines, and boys hauling buckets of water from the few pumps scattered throughout tent city. Francine waved goodbye as she ducked into her tent.

Paul reached his tent next and took a long whiff of his ma's cooking. "Hmmm! I'm starving. See ya later!" he smiled and disappeared into the tent.

Maggie slowed to a walk to catch her breath and was just about to her tent when she felt a tug on her sleeve.

"Now aw you weady to play ante ova?" said a little voice. Clara looked up with pleading eyes that blinked every time a raindrop landed on her forehead.

"Have you had lunch yet?" she asked Clara, who nodded yes. "Then I'd love to play, even if it is pouring!" she laughed. "Come on!"

Chapter 9
Illness and Injury

"Over here!" yelled the man on horseback. "Hook that cable up tighter. Steady, now. Okay, now straighten her up and pull her out!"

Paul watched the bulldozer drag their tent onto skids. What few belongings they had, including the upright piano, had been tied down on a nearby horse-drawn wagon. He listened intently as the man gave orders, then noticed the other man on the bulldozer push levers and pull knobs to make the machine turn, lift, and pull.

I wanna learn how to drive one of those. It doesn't look that hard. Think of all the things I could do on our land if we had one of those!

Just like the metal track of the bulldozer, the wheels were going around in Paul's head. He could see himself moving dirt, felling trees, pulling stumps and other fun things.

Without warning a cable slipped from the bottom of the tent frame and flew back, narrowly missing the driver. The tent swiveled off the skids and boards cracked as the frame twisted. Part of the tent collapsed on Pa who had put his arm out to protect himself. He yelled in agony and dropped to his knees under the weight of the tent. Ma, who had been standing by the wagon with the girls, screamed, and the man on the horse hollered, which made the horse rear up. For a second it seemed like total mayhem.

Quickly, the driver turned the machine off and jumped down. Paul and the men managed to lift the tent frame off Pa, who held his right arm in pain. Ma stood with her hands over her mouth, frozen, as if in shock.

"I think it's broke," Pa groaned as he held it up to look at it.

"Yep, I'd say yer prob'ly right," said the driver matter-of-factly.

Pa's arm was slanted down at a grotesque angle that made everyone grimace.

That has to hurt! Paul felt a little queasy.

"Come on, Henry," Ma said in a shaky voice, finally pulling herself together. "Let's see if we can find that doctor that came here with the transient workers."

"Paul, show the men where to put the tent and our belongings, would ya?" said Pa through clenched teeth.

Ma took Paul aside. "Paul, can you take Minnie back with you? I'm going to have the doctor look at Clara while we're there. She woke up with a bit of a fever and I'm afraid she might be coming down with something. Just keep an eye on Minnie till I get back." Ma looked worried and worn.

Poor Ma. If it's not one thing it's another!

"Sure, Ma, don't you worry. I'll make sure everything's okay." Paul shivered as he thought about the weird angle of Pa's arm when he held it up.

Within two hours the tent had been relocated to Camp 8 and everyone was busy unloading the wagon to put things back inside. The men grunted and groaned as they carried the piano inside. Minnie was tired and fell asleep as soon as her cot was laid out. Because it was late in the day, the driver parked the dozer off to the edge of the woods near the Jacobses' tent for the night. Paul watched him climb up on the wagon with the other worker and head back to the warehouse.

After checking on Minnie to make sure she was still asleep, Paul crept quietly out of the tent. Having a bulldozer parked outside his door was just too tempting. He walked around the big machine and felt the cold, hard, metal cleats of the track. No one seemed to be watching so he climbed up onto the seat.

Now this is something. It can't be that hard to operate this old girl. He touched a couple of levers and pretended to push this, make it turn, pick up dirt, lift the blade. He was totally engrossed in moving make-believe piles of dirt.

"You supposed to be up there?" came a stern, deep voice from behind.

Paul nearly jumped out of his skin. He turned to see who had caught him.

"Erik! You devil. You nearly scared me to death!" Paul breathed a sigh of relief.

"How'd you like my authoritative voice?" Erik laughed so hard he was doubled over. "Aw, I done the same thing the other day. Wouldn't it be something to drive one of these monsters?"

"Yeah, and I'm going to someday!" nodded Paul. "You just wait and see!"

"I bet you will," laughed Erik. "But right now I got to show you somethin'! It's our secret. I discovered it this afternoon while waitin' for you to move. Come down here!"

Curiosity got the better of Paul and he leaped off the tractor and onto the grass. Erik led him into the bushes. There, lying on the ground, was the biggest fish Paul had ever seen.

"Holy smokes, Erik!" he exclaimed. "Talk about a monster! What is it? It's as big as Minnie!"

"This here's a huge salmon. Can you believe it? And they're running in the river right now. I know where a great hole is. You won't believe it till you see it! And what a fight! Must weigh about forty pounds, don't you think?"

"At least!"

"Well, what are we waitin' for? Let's go!"

Paul hesitated. "I can't right now, much as I want to. I'm watchin' Minnie while Pa's at the doc. Think he broke his arm."

"You're kidding, right?" He followed Paul into the tent.

"I wish!" Paul tried to whisper so as not to wake Minnie up. He put a kettle of water on the stove and lit the fire. "I don't know what we're gonna do if Pa can't use his right arm to help with everything that needs to be done!"

"Wow, that's bad news!"

He and Erik sat on a makeshift bench outside the tent discussing fishing trips and other adventures they wanted to take along the rivers and up into the mountains. Finally, Paul heard a truck pull up by the end of the tent row and the familiar voices of his family. Paul and Erik ran to meet them.

Ma handed Clara to Paul, who laid her on her cot and covered her with a blanket. He felt her forehead. "She's burnin' up, Ma."

"I know. She's got the measles. Take the blanket off her for now. We'll just have to watch her and wait till her fever breaks." Lines of worry creased Ma's face as she put a cool cloth on Clara's forehead.

Pa shuffled over to his cot, his arm in a sling, and groaned in pain as he lay down.

"They had to straighten the bone back into place. I'm surprised you couldn't hear Pa scream way out here," Ma said sympathetically. "It'll be a little while before the medicine starts working, then you'll feel better, Henry. Try to get some sleep."

"Bless you boys for having some water ready for a cup of tea. Nothin' sounds better right now. You want some, Henry?"

Pa shook his head.

Erik headed for the door. "Well, let me know if there's anything I can do to help. I'm sure my pa will be over here tomorrow to see how things are going." He turned to Paul as he stepped down out of the tent. "Better get my monster fish to Ma. She's got some cannin' to do tonight!" He whistled as he headed in the direction of the fish he had hidden in the weeds.

Suddenly Erik let out a cry of dismay. They could hear him running back toward the tent.

"Somebody stole my fish!" he announced as he put his head back inside the door.

Paul jumped up and followed Erik to the scene of the crime.

"Well, I'm no detective, but here's a footprint right over here in the mud. Come look." he motioned to Erik.

"That looks like—why it looks like—"

"A bear!" they said in unison.

They ran back to tell the family that a bear had taken off with Erik's prize salmon that weighed as much as Minnie.

"You mean a bear was that close to our tent?" exclaimed Ma. She put her hand up to her forehead in disbelief.

"I forgot to tell you, Mary," said Pa, slurring his words now that the medicine had begun to take effect. "I saw a little black bear by the ladies' outhouse the other day. He seemed more afraid of me than I did of him, and he took off. Don't think it's anything you have to be afraid of."

"Ohhh," groaned Ma. "You seem to forget to tell me an awful lot of important things, Henry! I'll never be able to go to the outhouse alone again, much less let the girls go. And they are out playing in the woods all the time!" The more Ma thought about it the more upset she got.

"As long as there's noise and people around, he won't be anywhere near," Pa's voice started to fade. "He's just a little black bear." He mumbled something else but by then he was sound asleep.

Paul and Erik ran back out to see if they could find any other clues about where the bear had gone. Since Pa said it was a little one, they weren't too worried about running into it. Its trail was easy to follow until it got to the river; then they lost it.

Paul was just coming back inside the tent when he heard his ma quietly playing a tune on the piano. Tears ran down her face while she played, and she didn't notice Paul at first.

"It's gonna be okay, Ma," Paul said quietly as he stood beside her and put his hand on her shoulder. "Things are going to work out, you'll see."

Ma put her hand on top of his and nodded. "Between your Pa being hurt, Clara being sick, and now bears out there, I don't know what I'll do. But, as long as I can count on you, I know it'll be fine," she said.

Paul lay awake in his cot for a long time that night.

Pa and Ma need me, especially now. I have to take care of things. He rolled over in the bed and sighed. *Well, I took care of the family when Pa was travelin' and trying to find work back in Minnesota. Guess it won't be much different way up here.*

But it was different way up here. Life was very different. He felt a heavy weight on him, a responsibility that he wasn't sure he could handle. But he had to. He needed to stay strong. Somehow.

Chapter 10
A New Cemetery

Maggie had a sad look on her face as she and Mother sat on the step of the tent and watched several more colonists' tents being loaded onto skids and dragged away. Her family was going to be doing the same thing once the dozer was available. With only a few bulldozers owned by ARRC, they seemed to run from sunup to sundown hauling tents to various camps throughout the Matanuska Valley. As more and more colonists moved, the main camp grew quieter.

She looked at the empty holes around tent city.

"It'll never be the same," Maggie sighed.

"I know." Mother brushed Maggie's bangs with her fingers. "These past few weeks of playing and exploring with new friends on long summer days are about to change, aren't they?"

Maggie couldn't sleep that night. A mosquito had found its way into the tent and, just as she would doze off, would buzz past her ear then go silent. She'd wake up and lie there, waiting to feel the sting of it biting her somewhere. Dreams of a giant mosquito landing on the tent and trying to drill a hole in the ceiling with its huge stinger wove in and out of her consciousness. Someone was crying, and distant voices grew louder.

Suddenly Maggie sat upright in her cot. The voices were real, and came from the next tent over. "I'm so sorry, Myrna. He was such a sweet little thing," said a familiar voice.

"That's Mother!" thought Maggie aloud. Muffled sobs were now uncontrollable.

Maggie scrambled out of the cot, wrapped her wool blanket

around her and tiptoed barefoot to the next tent. The soft glow of the kerosene lamp showed Mother sitting next to Mrs. Evans, who was bent over sobbing. Mother gently stroked her back.

"It's got to be very hard," she was saying softly.

"Maggie, is that you?" Mother noticed her standing there. "Little Daniel died tonight, Maggie. The doctor thinks it was complications of the measles." She could tell her mother was trying to stay strong, though Maggie could see she, too, had been crying.

"Daniel?" repeated Maggie. There was a catch in her throat and the name came out hoarsely. Shivers ran up her body, though she didn't know if it was from the shock of the news or the chill of the night-time air. Everyone knew several children were sick throughout camp, but— "He died?" she repeated.

"Maggie." Mother's voice brought her back to reality. "Since you're up, please go fill the bucket with water from the pump. I think Myrna would feel better with a cup of hot tea."

Maggie stumbled numbly between the row of tents and down the path, clutching the gray scratchy blanket with one hand and the bucket with the other. The sky was still bright though it was the middle of the night. Reverend Bingle from church had explained last Sunday that today was the summer solstice, the longest day of the year.

A tear rolled down Maggie's cheek. She raised and lowered the cold pump handle slowly, trying not to let the noisy squeaks wake people up. The bucket was heavy, and freezing cold water sloshed out and down her leg as she walked up the gentle slope of the path. By the time she reached the Evanses' tent it was half gone, but Mother thanked her and poured what was left into the kettle. Mr. Evans had returned from the hospital, and his wife was calmer as she rocked gently in the chair with her eyes closed. Silent tears slid steadily down her cheeks. Her husband sat quietly beside her while Mother set about making tea.

"Try to go back to bed now, Maggie," she said softly. "It'll be a hard day tomorrow and you'll need your sleep."

As Maggie crawled back into her cot, she heard the buzzing of the mosquito overhead.

"Oh, no," she moaned. She pulled the blanket up over her head and, after a few more tears thinking of Daniel, soon fell asleep.

Except for mothers caring for sick children, nearly everyone came for Daniel's funeral. One of the men had made a little coffin out of pine boards, which was carried on the back of an ARRC truck. Men, women, and children followed solemnly as the truck wound along the rough, bumpy road to the newly chosen cemetery. Four-year-old Daniel was the first to be buried there.

The reverend led the sad ceremony. Mrs. Evans wept openly and had to be helped back to the truck when it was over. Erik left with his pa to help Mr. Evans. The sun was warm and the air still as the smell of fresh dirt mingled with wildflowers. Paul, Maggie, and Francine stayed behind to lay wild shasta daisies on Daniel's grave. Paul was very quiet and deep in thought as he stood looking at the new mound of earth.

"Watcha thinking?" asked Maggie quietly.

Paul didn't answer for a while. "About life, I guess," he finally said, shrugging his shoulders. "About how little Daniel traveled all the way up here like the rest of us only to get sick and die. Just doesn't seem right."

Maggie didn't say anything for a few moments but looked at Paul and the flowers and the grave.

"We were playing catch a few days ago," she mumbled as she picked the petals off a daisy. "How could he be dead?" She looked at Paul. "I've never known anyone who died before except Grandpa, but I was too little to remember."

"He was just a little kid." Paul didn't seem to hear Maggie. "It don't seem fair! What if Clara dies? She's sick with the measles right now." A tear rolled down his cheek. Embarrassed, he quickly wiped it with his sleeve. Before he could let more tears fall, he turned and walked back toward camp with long, angry strides.

Maggie and Francine stood and watched a group of small children laughing and chasing each other. "Look at them playing over there. They don't even understand."

"Life is so simple to a child," Francine whispered.

"Mother was right, it has been a very hard day," Maggie sighed as she watched Paul disappear over a hill.

Chapter 11
Fannie

Paul walked hard and fast a longer route back to Camp 8. He needed to be alone, to think. He remembered feeling this way when Pa wouldn't let him bring Rascal.

This wasn't how I thought it would be, moving up here. Ma's unhappy, Pa's hurt, Clara's sick, and now little Daniel died! His fists were clenched in frustration as his feet pounded the earth. *It's not fair!*

It was at least an hour before Paul had calmed down enough to go back to the tent. Belle wagged her tail as he opened the tent flap and came in. She seemed to be trying to cheer him up. His frown turned to a smile as he bent down to scratch her under the chin. "I'm so glad you're living with us now, you little whippersnapper!"

He bent over Clara as she slept and felt her forehead.

"How's she doing?"

"Still pretty warm," Ma sighed. "But at least she's not gettin' worse."

"Here's some lunch." She set a bowl of soup and biscuits on the table. "Your pa would like you to hitch Fannie up and meet him at the property. They've just cut some trees and need her to drag them to the burn pile. I'll send some lunch for him, too." Ma sat down and studied Paul's face. "You doing okay? It's been a sad morning, hasn't it?" she said tenderly.

"I'm okay, Ma," said Paul, trying not to look at her for fear his emotions would get the better of him again.

He inhaled his lunch, grabbed his cap, and set out to get Fannie harnessed up.

Well, the funeral is over and it's life as usual. Men aren't supposed to show emotion, remember?

Fannie was a big white horse that had been shipped up for the colonists. Rumor was she had earned her name by sitting down on her rear end at the shipyard in Seattle and refusing to board. So men simply built a crate around her and hoisted her onto the ship. Though stubborn about going to sea, she was a faithful workhorse for the Jacobses. As hard as they pushed her, she'd work all day and still be ready to go again in the morning.

Fannie saw him coming and whinnied as he approached the fenced area near Camp 8 that held her and a few other horses. "You ready to do some serious pullin', old girl?" She snorted and bobbed her head up and down. "I do believe that was a yes," he chuckled. She was soon harnessed up and heading out to the property.

Paul heard the chopping of axes and the zzzip zzzap of crosscut saws against wood long before he spotted Pa and the other men. As transient workers cleared the land, logs were dragged into piles and rows to be burned later. Jagged outlines of logs, treetops, and brush lay like scars across the landscape.

Paul stopped Fannie to survey their progress. *Looks like they got most of the trees cleared for the house, but there's an awful lot left!*

Despite his broken arm, Pa still oversaw the operation. Up at four in the morning, home around six at night, he'd grab some dinner, collapse in the cot, and do it again the next day. "Daylight's a-wastin'!" he'd say. "I'm not about to sit around doin' nothing."

"Paul!" hollered Pa when he caught sight of him riding Fannie bareback through the trees. "You're just in time! We need Fannie over here. Shorty, grab that cable there and wrap it around the end," he hollered to one of the transient workers. Though Pa's arm was in a cast, he could still give directions.

Paul helped as they hooked Fannie up to the end of the log, wrapped and tightened the cable, and lightly smacked her rear end. She leaned into the harness, snorted, pulled, and dug her hooves into the soft ground. The muscles of her legs and rump rippled. Mosquitoes buzzed around her eyes and ears, as if to torment her. The log slid little by little along the spongy ground called tundra. Sweat dripped down her neck and sides as she breathed heavily while the log was unhitched and hoisted end over end onto the burn pile. All afternoon one log after another met a similar fate.

"That's enough for today, fellas," Pa wiped the sweat from his face with a handkerchief. Including Erik's father and older brother, there was Mr. Engles, their neighbor, and two transients helping. "I'll see if we can rent the dozer from Mr. Irwin to pull out these stumps in the next few days."

"Can we meet at my place tomorrow, then?" asked Mr. Engles. They all nodded and headed back to camp, tired and hungry.

I'm glad I don't have to help every day. That's some hard work!

Paul led Fannie by the reins on their way back to camp, about a half mile away. Every now and then she'd snatch a mouthful of grass along the trail. A horn honked as a truck bumped along past them. Everyone waved.

"Sure would be nice to have one of those," murmured Paul.

"Yeah, well, it'll be a while afore any of us colonists can afford one! Rate we're goin' we'll be lucky to have a house to live in, no matter what the government promised us. Danged arm! Now they're lettin' us help and I'm in a cast!"

Paul looked over at Pa. It was the first time he'd heard him sound discouraged. He didn't know what to say.

"I think we've got enough land cleared for the house, the barn and maybe a garden," Pa went on. "Just runnin' out of time. They say it can start gettin' cold in September and October up here, and it's already late June. Sure don't want to be livin' in that tent during the winter!"

Paul nodded in agreement, focused more on smacking mosquitoes. The evenings were the worst, after the breeze died down. He finally gave up, took a wadded-up piece of mosquito netting out of his pocket, and slipped it over his hat and face. He hated wearing it, but at least it kept the annoying bugs out of his eyes and mouth.

"Well," said Pa thoughtfully as they walked, "our problems are nothin' compared to the Evanses'. The good Lord has helped us so far, and it'll all work out. Gotta stay positive." He slapped Paul on the back making him wince, as usual.

"Have you seen the house plans your ma picked out yet?"

"No, I saw her looking at them," Paul was glad Pa changed the subject. "Which one did she pick?"

"Last I knew it was number four, though you know how she changes her mind. Good thing there are only five to chose from!" he laughed. "It's got two stories, so you and the girls will have your own rooms upstairs—"

Fannie suddenly stopped and pricked up her ears.

"Hey, Mr. Jacobs!" yelled a frantic voice from a field along the road. "Can you help us? Hurry, please! Come quick!"

Paul coaxed Fannie into a trot toward the pleading man. A young boy lay crying on the ground, his feet and lower legs wrapped in the man's shirt.

"He was out here playin' while I was burnin' these brush piles and he stepped in a hole. That danged tundra just smolders under there, but you can't tell to look at it." The man picked the sobbing boy up. "His feet are burned pretty bad. Can you help me take him to the doc?"

As he lifted the boy onto Fannie's back the shirt fell off to reveal blistered and burnt skin on his legs and feet. Paul groaned.

"We better get to town, quick," said Pa. "Come on, Fannie. Paul, run ahead and see if you can find the doctor. We'll meet you at the nurse's tent."

Paul felt new strength surge through his tired legs as he sprinted down the long stretch of rough road to town. The sight of the boy's injuries and the sound of his cries spurred him.

I've heard about kids gettin' burned. Just hope I can find that doc. He could be anywhere! he thought worriedly.

Paul finally reached the Red Cross nurse's tent. Miss DeForas, the only nurse for the whole valley, was bent over a sick child lying on a cot, taking her temperature and listening to her breathe. For a minute Paul thought it was Clara. He breathed a sigh of relief when it wasn't.

The nurse looked up when she was done and smiled. Everyone liked her. She was busy day and night and looked very tired. "Can I help you?"

"There's a little boy down the road, south. His feet are burned pretty bad. Do you know where the doc is?" Paul was out of breath as he tried to speak.

"He's in the Butte, and won't be back. He stays with the transients over there most of the time. Is the little boy on his way here?"

"Yeah, my pa's bringing him on our horse."

"I'll make room for him. Thank you for letting me know. There's not much we can do till he gets here." She bent down over the little girl and put a cool rag on her forehead.

"Would you mind fetching me some more water—I'm sorry, I don't know your name," she smiled her sweet smile again.

"It's Paul. And sure, I'll be right back." For once he didn't mind hauling water.

Chapter 12
Fourth of July

A picnic with wooden benches and tables placed here and there near the train station was all the celebration for the Fourth of July that first summer. Though most had gathered for the funeral a few days earlier, no one had socialized. Today everyone was happy to see each other, despite the mud.

Paul, Erik, and a few other boys ran around with American flags. Paul stopped by a little boy with bandaged feet sitting on his father's shoulders and gave him a flag. He had a huge smile when he saw Paul.

"Henry, I heard about your arm. How you been?" greeted a colonist they hadn't seen for a while. "How's your land coming along?" or "Have they started on your house yet?" or "Isn't it a shame about the little Evans boy?" or "Did you hear nine families done left yesterday? Just couldn't handle it, I guess," went the conversations.

Paul, Maggie, Erik, and Francine sat together as they shared a pine bench and soaked up the sunshine. They reminisced about Fourth of July parades and picnics back home.

"Seems strange to not have much of a celebration," noted Erik as he devoured a plate of food.

"Well, everything's different up here, and with people having so much to worry about, I guess no one's had time to organize anything," said Francine.

"Yeah, it has been pretty strange, and so sad with three little boys dying. I'm glad Clara's feeling better," Maggie said cheerfully, hoping to lighten the conversation.

"Yeah, her fever broke yesterday and she's making up for lost time!" Paul smiled as he watched her laughing and playing with the other children.

"Thank goodness!" said Maggie. "I see our mothers found each other."

They watched as the two women greeted each other with a hug and big smiles.

"How are you, Helen?" said Mary, Paul's ma, as they sat down on a bench to eat. "I see you finally got your tent moved out here to Camp 8, and I've been wanting to visit with you."

"Oh, we're much better now that William can work," chuckled Helen. "He's a lot easier to live with! It drove him crazy to sit and wait on the transient workers, which drove me crazy!" She laughed. "How are things going for you, Mary?" Helen knew that Mary still missed her family in Minnesota.

"Well, I'm trying," she lifted her eyes to Helen with a slight smile. "I heard from my folks the other day and they're doing well. They say the drought is worse than ever this year and it was a good thing we left when we did." She glanced around to make sure the girls hadn't strayed too far. "At least Clara's over the measles. I was terribly worried about her."

"Yes, I can imagine! And I'm sure it was very hard leaving family. I was never that close with my kin, so it's not so difficult. How do you like living in a tent for so long?" she smiled, knowingly.

"It's no picnic, is it?" replied Mary. Both women laughed. "My lands, it's a lot of work; hauling water, washing clothes by hand, cooking on those coal stoves. When you think about it, that's what we did back home!" They laughed again.

"Amen to that!" replied Helen. "Did you hear gasoline-powered washing machines are supposed to be here any day? Won't that be living in luxury?"

"Well, not quite luxury, but a little closer!" Mary laughed. "It'll just give me more time to can the fish Paul keeps bringing home!"

"Fish, grouse, ptarmigan, rabbits! Heavens, this place is full of all kinds of animals that end up in my pressure cooker," sighed Helen. "We have enough food to last for years!"

Clara and Minnie brought little bouquets of lupine and wild geraniums to each of the mothers.

"Thank you, girls, these are lovely." They both smiled.

"How's Henry getting by with his broken arm?" Helen asked.

"Oh, he's not the most pleasant person to be around right now. We had to go into Anchorage to see the doctor. It was a pretty bad break. He said it'd be another month till the cast can come off—if he's careful."

"That'll be into August!" said Helen.

"Yes, and there's so much to be done." Mary took a deep breath. "Henry tells me to stop worrying so much."

Helen leaned over and patted Mary's arm. "Well, try not to, Mary. There are lots of folks that can help. Let's just enjoy the day. See, there's Paul over there with Michael and Maggie playing ball. It looks like they're having a great time."

Everyone had a wonderful day, and enjoyed a break from the chores of daily life.

The following day it was back to work. The Coopers had rounded up five extra transients and neighbors to show up at the Jacobses' home site. Even Erik came with his pa. They all helped clear stumps and haul them to the burn piles. The site was close to being ready to start building their little house. Paul and Erik usually played more than worked, but today they helped right alongside the others. Everyone felt a spirit of cooperation that was contagious.

Pa put his good arm around Ma's shoulder and held her close as they watched the activity in amazement. "This is our family now," he said. "Our kinfolk are back in Minnesota, but our new family is right here helpin' each other."

Ma smiled and nodded.

Toward evening the familiar clang of Ma's cast-iron frying pan rang out. "Time for some grub!" Pa announced as they finished up and headed for the Jacobses' tent.

"Come on in!" insisted Ma. "It's nothing fancy, but there's plenty for everyone. Dig in, fellas!"

Everyone noticed how happy Ma seemed. Paul glanced at Pa and they both smiled.

Steaming beef stew and thick slices of homemade bread were devoured amidst laughter and joking.

"Well, Henry," said Shorty. "I think you're ready to have them stumps pulled by the dozer. We done tried to chop 'em out, but those roots don't go down, they go out—way out!"

"I swear that ground is still frozen in places," said another transient.

"I believe it," laughed Pa. "This Alaskan soil don't want to give up anything without a fight!"

Just then a voice was heard at the tent door. Everyone turned to look.

"Excuse me, folks," said a gentleman looking very much out of place with a camera slung over his shoulder and a fancy jacket on. "I was riding past and happened to hear some happy conversation from this direction. Mind if I join you for a bit?"

"Ain't you that reporter from Wisconsin we see ridin' yer horse up and down 'round here?" asked Pa.

Paul could visualize the man flying down the road on his horse, his camera flopping up and down and his long coattails flying out behind him, always in a hurry to get his story on the next train.

"That's me," he smiled. "Name's Schalaben." He shook hands all around as Ma took some clothes off a cot so he could sit down.

"Can I get you some supper, Mr. Schalaben?" she asked.

"Why, I didn't realize it was suppertime," he looked at his fancy watch. "Never do seem to know what time it is with these long days. But it sure does smell mighty good. Thank you!" He almost drooled as Ma handed him a bowl.

"So you're writing articles about this colony project?" Erik asked.

"Yes I am, young man. Came up on the train and boat with the Michigan and Wisconsin folks and have been here ever since. Fascinating! I write for the *Milwaukee Journal*."

"Well, there's no shortage of things to write about," said Pa. "Lots of colonists are more than happy to let the whole world know how bad things are up here."

"Yes, I've heard a lot of that. And a lot of reporters like to write that kind of news, too. But like I say, I've been here the whole time and I believe in reporting the truth." He pointed at Pa with his spoon to emphasize the word truth.

Everyone in the tent watched with interest as he hungrily gobbled up his food as though he hadn't eaten in a while. When he finally looked up and realized he was the center of attention, he blushed.

"Sorry," he licked his fingers and patted his mouth with a napkin. "Delicious! Now, what were we saying?"

"You told us you believe in reportin' the truth," said Pa.

"Ah, yes. Well, let me ask you a few questions, if you don't mind." He took a pad and pencil out of his jacket pocket. "You're just the sort of folks I've been looking for."

"Now, what would you say has been the hardest part of this whole project?" he looked around, his pencil ready to write.

"Leavin' kinfolk!" Ma blurted out.

"So, it's not living in a tent like this, possibly until winter sets in?" he looked at Ma.

"No," she shook her head. "This ain't all that bad."

"It's not the mosquitoes or the mud or the frustration with government rules, or …"

"No, it's none of those things," chuckled Erik's pa. "Though they have been a challenge."

"Well then, what else would you all say is the hardest thing, besides leaving family?"

He looked around at the weathered faces of the men and women, and the earnest faces of the youngsters, all who had set out to succeed at a new life in a raw land.

"Not givin' up, even when things seem impossible," Paul said firmly.

Everyone turned and looked at Paul, then exploded with cheers and applause.

Pa patted him on the back. "Amen to that!" he laughed, and they all repeated, "Amen!"

Chapter 13
Tomlinson's Cabin

"What do ya wanna do today?" Erik asked as he chewed on a long piece of grass.

Paul, Maggie, and Erik all sat on the bench in front of Paul's tent, enjoying the sun after a few days of drizzly rain. Belle was curled up under Paul's feet, as usual.

"Get rid of these mosquitoes!" exclaimed Maggie as she smacked one biting her on the arm. "Ever since the rain stopped, there seem to be millions more!"

"Don't you have yer head net?" Paul asked as he put his on under his hat.

"Yeah, I have it, but I hate it," Maggie said, disgusted.

"Why, I've never heard such negative words come out of your mouth, Maggie Cooper!" Paul said with a sarcastic smile.

"Oh, I can be very negative when it comes to mosquitoes!"

"You guys done any explorin' down that way, past the water pump?" Erik pointed toward the woods between Camp 8 and the Matanuska River, about a mile away.

"No, haven't had much time for that." Paul's face lit up. "Wanna go?"

"Let's go!" Maggie jumped up, which startled Belle who nearly knocked Paul off the bench.

"Whoa," laughed Paul. "I guess we're going! I'll let Ma know."

The three explorers followed the path past the water pump toward Tomlinson Lake, a favorite swimming hole for kids in Camp 8. Laughter could be heard as they neared the lake.

"Hi, Catherine!" Maggie waved. "How's the water?"

"Freezing, but fun!" Catherine yelled back as she splashed her little sister. Her mother, Margaret, who had had dinner with the Jacobses that first night in the Valley, waved and smiled.

Not far past the lake they came to a fork in the path. "Well, which one should we take?" Erik grinned.

"How about the one to the right?" suggested Maggie. "It looks mysterious."

"Sounds good to me. Come on, girl!" Paul whistled to Belle, who had chased a small squirrel up a tree.

The trail was not easy to walk on. Thick brush, devil's club with huge thorns, and trees knocked over by the wind were constant obstacles. Despite swarms of mosquitoes that encircled them, they cheerfully tromped up and down small hills, deeper into the woods.

"Maybe this is an animal trail, though it looks pretty well used," said Erik.

"Look at all the pretty little flowers." Maggie bent over to inspect some small white blossoms when she noticed something partially buried in the brush. "Look, isn't that an old pail or something?" She pointed to something metal a few feet off the path.

"Yep, it's a bucket." Erik went over to examine it more closely.

"Well, didn't the name Tomlinson Lake come from the homesteader who settled here a while back?" Paul started thinking about bits and pieces of conversations he'd heard.

"I heard that, too," said Erik. "Our fathers were talking about that one day now that you mention it."

"Well, there must be a cabin or something around here, then," said Maggie excitedly.

"Maybe the old man still lives back in here!"

"Naw, I heard the government bought up all this land for the colonists," said Erik.

"Besides, we'd have seen folks comin' and goin', don't ya think?"

"Look! Isn't that a clearing—through the woods up ahead?" Paul pointed.

They all stopped to look.

"Well, this path seems to head right for it," Maggie whispered.

Indeed, the path opened up into a clearing dotted with old stumps.

"Look at that little cabin. It's smaller than our tents!" Paul laughed. "And that must've been the garden," he waved his arm over an area that had once been mounded rows but were now blooms of purple fireweed and white cow parsnip.

"He was trying to clear this all by hand!" Erik said. "That must've been slow going! Think how hard it is with several men and horses, not to mention bulldozers!"

"No kidding! And he didn't get too far. Looks like only a few acres were cleared all together," Paul answered. "Look at all the tools lyin' around."

"Let's go check the cabin out," Maggie started in that direction across the field.

"Be careful," warned Paul, but Maggie didn't wait.

"A little worried about her?" Erik teased him.

"Well, you never know what's around here. Could be snakes …"

"Nope, ain't no snakes in Alaska."

"Really? You sure?"

"Yep. Heard it right from Mr. Irwin himself."

"Well, much as I like snakes, it don't break my heart if there ain't any here. Bears are bad enough!"

Paul and Erik stopped talking and looked across the field at Maggie, suddenly aware that a bear could wander out into the opening as they spoke.

"Maggie! Wait!" Paul started running toward her, with Erik right behind. "We've got to stay together."

"Well, you guys are just standing there, and I want to see what's in this cabin!" she put her hands on her hips impatiently.

"Yeah, your mother mentioned your dangerous curiosity not too long ago!" laughed Paul.

Maggie wrinkled up her face. "Well, are you coming?'

"Just remember, Maggie," Erik held up his hand. "There are bears around here, and you just can't go trompin' off by yourself! Okay?"

"Okay, I promise," she held up her right hand. "Now are you ready?"

They crept up the well-worn path to the tiny cabin, quietly stepping over rusted tools and equipment.

"Don't think anyone lives here, do you?" Paul whispered.

Maggie shook her head. "All the windows are boarded up. Maybe the front door's open."

Erik reached the front door first. "Would ya look at that!" he scratched his head. A scribbled note on weathered paper was tacked to the front door:

Private Property!
Open this door and you'll find a loaded gun in your face!

"Do you think someone's in there?" Maggie whispered with a shocked expression on her face as she shrank away from the door.

"Naw, couldn't be," Erik said, somewhat hesitantly.

"Well, is it a hoax?" she said.

"I bet it is," said Paul. He proceeded to knock loudly on the door. "Hey, anyone there!"

Maggie put her hands over her mouth as if to stifle a scream in case someone answered from inside. Then she started giggling.

"What's so funny?" Erik wondered, somewhat serious.

"You should see the look on your faces!" she tried to laugh quietly. "I think you're both scared to death!"

"Me? I'm not scared! Why, I'm gonna open this door right now and show you …"

"Oh, no you're not!" Paul blocked him from touching the door. "If the stories I heard about ol' Tomlinson are true, figuring out a way to get a gun to go off when the door opens is right up his alley."

"Well," Erik backed off a little and started to think. "What if we lie down and push the door open with a long stick or something?"

"Yeah, but if it's a shotgun, those pellets'll go everywhere," said Paul. "We could still get hit!"

They sat on a log near the cabin and talked at length about whether to go in, and if so, how.

Suddenly, a huge black raven flew overhead and landed on the roof above the door. Its loud raucous rantings and ravings seemed to be directed at the three youngsters.

"I'm going to take that as an omen that we should leave well enough alone," Paul murmured under his breath. "Maybe there's a dead body in there or somethin'."

"Yeah, Natives believe ravens are spirits that have messages for people," agreed Erik. "I think I got the message!"

"Let's go!" Maggie started across the field to the path. "Someone needs to make sure I don't run into a bear!" she yelled back over her shoulder.

Paul ran after her with Erik following behind, shaking his head.

"He must be in love," Erik mumbled to Belle, who trotted past. "Well, that was an exciting adventure, wasn't it girl?"

Belle stopped to scratch her neck with her back foot, then ran on after Paul.

"I'll take that as a yes."

Chapter 14
The New Doctor

"Congratulations, Mrs. Vanders. You have a beautiful little girl! The first colony baby born in the Matanuska Valley!" smiled Miss DeForas. She and Dr. Ostrum, the transient workers' doctor, stood beside the happy new mother, holding the newborn for a photographer.

The smile was genuine, but Miss DeForas was exhausted. So many children were sick, and three little boys had already died. Expectant women were starting to have their babies. One nurse couldn't be everywhere at once, and Dr. Ostrum was mainly there for the workers.

Many colonists were angry at the government for not thinking ahead about providing medical care. One mother took matters into her own hands. She wrote a letter to the First Lady, Mrs. Eleanor Roosevelt herself, explaining how children were sick and dying and there was no doctor to take care of them.

It wasn't long before the problem was solved.

"Hullo?" said a man's tired voice as he picked up the phone late one night from his room in Anchorage. "You want me to go where? When?" Dr. C. Earl Albrecht asked. "The Matanuska Valley—tonight?"

"Yes, tonight," said Dr. Joseph Romig. "Things are bad. You need to get out there tonight and take care of those colonists. Children are sick, there have been three deaths, and the people are frantic. Mrs. Roosevelt even sent up an investigating team from Washington that's insisting we do something immediately!"

"This is just a temporary assignment, right?" Dr. Albrecht asked.

He wanted to work with Alaska Natives in rural villages, not with colonists in the Matanuska Valley.

"You can go to the villages later," was Dr. Romig's reply.

Around two o'clock the next morning Dr. Albrecht and three nurses, along with whatever supplies they could round up, pulled into the Matanuska Station in the Speeder car, Colonel Olson's special car outfitted with locomotive wheels. The doctor was surprised to see colonists waiting at that hour.

"Say doc, are we ever glad to see you!" said a relieved father.

The only hospital had been a tent. Now, carpenters were busy hammering and sawing through the night to turn the Community Center into the new hospital. Sheets were hung from the ceiling to separate beds, two woodstoves burned, cots were brought in, and the first patient, a little boy with asthma and measles, was admitted at five o'clock a.m.

"Here, Doc." said Max Sherrod, as he set a big pot on a table. "Dorothy says you can use our pressure cooker to sterilize the instruments. I'll go get more wood for the fire."

Max and Dorothy Sherrod, both nurses, had been hired to care for several sick kids traveling from Seattle to Alaska, but their job ended when the children reached the Valley. Now they both heartily helped the new medical team. With his thick glasses and eager smile, Max did whatever was needed, from chopping wood to rigging up barrels and pipes for water, and helping with surgeries. Dorothy cared for mothers with new babies.

Within a few hours, all ten beds were filled with sick children. Dr. Albrecht and his staff of nurses knew they'd be busy for a long time.

———

One evening, a few weeks later, Paul's family was eating supper in the tent. "Sorry Ma. I've got to go check on Fannie," Paul said suddenly, and he was out the door before Ma could swallow her food. Little Belle, who never left his side, raced off behind him. Two minutes later the familiar form of Dr. Albrecht filled the tent door.

"Evening, folks," he said in his low, calm voice. "I believe you have some young'uns that would be much better off without their tonsils.

Mind if I take them in to the hospital? I'll have them home by tomorrow afternoon." He smiled kindly.

It wasn't a request so much as a command.

"Are there balloons and ice cream?" the girls asked, excitedly. They had heard about treats for children who had their tonsils out.

"Oh yes, the nurses have a big party waiting for you," he winked and smiled.

"Minnie, Clara, go get your things, and mind the doctor. Now where in the world did Paul take off to?" wondered Ma.

Pa smiled, knowing that Paul had a constant ear out for the sound of Dr. Albrecht's old truck. It was common for the doctor or nurse to round up children to have their tonsils out by driving out to tent camps and homesites.

Paul ran to Erik's tent down the row to warn him. They both hid. Sure enough, the doctor stopped at the next tent. By the time he was done there were five children in the truck, laughing and looking forward to ice cream.

"If they only knew what they were in for!" whispered Paul. "No way am I havin' my tonsils out!"

"Me either!"

They laughed and headed back to their tents.

"They'll never catch me," Paul bragged as he sat back down at the table to finish supper.

"No, but I will," smiled Ma, holding something behind her back. "Open up! Whether or not you have your tonsils out, you'll be takin' this every day."

"No, not cod liver oil!" Paul made a sour face as Ma poured a big spoonful into his mouth.

"Ugh! That stuff is horrible!" he shivered as it went down.

Belle, who was sitting by Paul's chair, looked up and watched him take the medicine. When she saw his reaction, she quietly sneaked under a cot and lay down. She didn't want any of that stuff either!

Chapter 15
A Fishy Adventure

"Ready?" said Paul. He and Belle stood at the door of Maggie's tent. His curly blond hair stuck out from under a beat-up cap and his blue eyes lit up with anticipation. A fishing pole was slung over one shoulder and he had a burlap bag in the other hand. Erik walked up, and both stood with excited grins on their faces. Even Belle had a silly expression.

Maggie glanced at Erik, then Paul, then Belle and laughed. "I don't know what I'm getting into, but I'll be ready in a second." She disappeared into the tent, then poked her head back out. "Can David come too? Father said he could have the day off from clearing if it was okay with you."

"Course it's okay!" said Erik. "As long as he promises to keep my fishin' hole a secret!" he added in a serious tone.

"Hold on, we'll be right there. Mother's putting some lunch together. You did bring something to eat, didn't you?"

"Food?" Paul looked at Erik and they both shook their heads. "Hadn't even thought about that, we're so excited to go fishin'!" Paul took off his cap to shoe some mosquitoes away. "I got Buhach to keep mosquitoes away, and bait—what else do you need?"

"Mother thought that might be the case. She packed extra," Maggie smiled. "Bye!" she yelled over her shoulder as she and David jumped off the tent porch. "We'll be back by supper!" David had a gun over one shoulder and a fishing pole over the other.

"You plan on shootin' somethin', David?" teased Erik.

"Only if I have to," answered David.

The four headed toward Tomlinson Lake, took the trail around it, and came to the Matanuska River.

"Are we crossing the river?" Maggie was suddenly suspicious that this outing was more than a simple hike to a fishing hole.

"Oh, did I forget to mention that part?" Erik had an innocent look on his face.

"Do you want to head back, Maggie? Now's the time," teased Paul. "Once you get across there's no turnin' back!"

"Is that a dare?" she asked.

"It'll be fine," David reassured them. "I've crossed it before. What Mother doesn't know won't kill her!"

The Matanuska River, like many Alaskan rivers, wound through the landscape like strands of spaghetti. One year the river might wind in one direction, the next year a different one. The river bed could be a mile wide, but the channel of water itself might be only thirty feet across. They managed to find a section of the river that wasn't too deep and had enough rocks to step on. Fortunately, no one fell in the ice-cold water.

An hour later four tired youngsters walked the last of Erik's secret animal trail that ended at Jim Creek. A short distance away was shallow marshy Jim Lake that sat at the foot of the Chugach Mountains. Past it loomed Knik Glacier, which had carved the valley out many centuries before.

As they plopped down on the bank a sudden long low mournful cry from the direction of the lake broke the silence.

"Look!" pointed Maggie. "What kind of bird is that?"

"It's a loon," said David. "Pretty much every lake has a pair. Don't they sound eerie?"

They all watched a large black and white bird with a checkered ring around its neck dive and surface near the edge of the lake, not far from the headwaters of the creek.

"Listen," Paul cocked his head. "That must be the female answering from across the lake."

They listened to the sad-sounding cries back and forth between the two loons. Belle started howling, too.

"I'm glad it's not dark," shivered Maggie. "They sound like they're crying because someone died! It gives me goosebumps!"

"Look down there! Now that gives me goosebumps!" Erik motioned toward the creek as he got his fishing line ready. "Have you ever seen a sight like that?"

"Wow!" whistled David. "So this is your secret hole. Look at all them fish!"

The water rippled with long, sleek, silver fish heading up the creek to the lake. Everyone quickly baited their hooks, spread out along the bank, and cast into the clear, cold water.

"Havin' some trouble casting there, sis?" teased David.

Maggie kept getting her line tangled up with Paul's and was getting frustrated.

"No," she answered defensively. "I'm just not too good at casting yet."

Paul walked over to try to untangle it for the fifth time, but Maggie gave him a look that said "I can do it myself, thank you!" so he let her untangle it. When she turned away, he looked at Erik, who was grinning from ear to ear.

An hour and a half later, tired from pulling so many fish in, they stopped for lunch.

Overcast and cool, Paul lit some of the Buhach powder to keep the swarms of mosquitoes away.

"Hmmmm. Sure glad your ma packed us lunch," said Erik as he wolfed down fried chicken and biscuits. "We'd a been pretty hungry, huh Paul?"

"Uh huh," smiled Paul, his mouth too full to talk.

Soon the clouds gave way to blue skies and a gentle breeze. The sound of the creek murmuring over and around boulders was soothing. Even Belle quit exploring and chasing squirrels to curl up in the sun and take a nap.

"Boy, I could almost take a little snooze myself," said Paul as he lay back on the bank and looked up at the sky. "Hey, look up, you guys."

A bald eagle soared majestically overhead, landing from treetop to treetop. The powerful whoosh of its huge graceful wings were breathtaking. Everyone oohed and aahed softly.

"With those mountains in the background, this could be a postcard!" whispered Maggie, not wanting to spoil the moment.

A loud snap of a branch came from the other side of the creek. Everyone bolted upright. Belle jumped up and growled. The hair stood up on the back of her neck.

"What was that?" Maggie crept closer to David.

"Stay still," whispered David as he slowly reached for his gun that leaned against a bush. "Look. Over there." He pointed to a spot upriver.

Thirty yards away, bushes swayed and rippled. More branches cracked. David slowly raised his gun and pointed it toward the noise. They all stared and held their breath.

Chapter 16
Bear!

With a great grunt, the big brown bear stood up on its hind legs. Its blond fur glowed in the sun as it sniffed the air and looked around. No one dared move except Belle who whimpered and ran over to Paul.

He must be seven feet tall! Paul thought as his heart beat wildly in his chest. *Look at the size of those paws, and those claws! Boy, I wish I had my gun, too. Lucky for us we're downwind—he must not know we're here. Whew! There he goes!*

Everyone breathed a sigh of relief as the bear finally fell down on all fours and lumbered away toward the lake. Smashed bushes and broken branches left a wide path.

"He's not gone yet!" whispered Maggie. The grizzly came back into view on the opposite bank. He stealthily walked into the water, watched for a moment, and with one sweep brought up a wriggling salmon in his gigantic paw. Putting the struggling fish in his mouth, he climbed back to shore, sat down to eat the fish in three or four bites, then ambled toward the lake.

David finally lowered his gun.

"He just needed a little snack," chuckled Erik nervously. "You know, I think I'm quite ready to head home. What about you guys?"

It only took a few seconds for everyone to gather their fish and head the opposite way for home!

As the distance between them and the bear increased, they recalled their close encounter and the adventures of the day with laughter and jokes, though each occasionally looked around to make sure there weren't any critters following them.

Erik tried to act silly as he skipped across rocks on the Matanuska River, and promptly fell into the cold water.

"Ha!" laughed Paul. "Serves you right for showing off! Good thing we're not far from home!"

Erik sloshed with every step as they giggled and joked the rest of the way.

"Here you go, Ma," said Paul with a tired but proud smile as he laid the sack full of salmon on the table.

Ma looked up from the letter she'd been writing to her folks back home. "I do declare," she sighed. "We'll have enough canned salmon to last a lifetime!"

"Speaking of food, when's supper? I'm starving!" he said as he sat down on the rough pine bench.

"Supper'll be ready in an hour. You'll just have to wait. Where did you catch these, son? You've been gone all day." She reached for the pressure cooker from a shelf above the coal- burning stove.

"Jim Creek," he answered.

"Land sakes. Way over there?" She looked Paul over. "And how in the world did you get so filthy?"

His clothes were wet and muddy. Black silt coated his boots, and streaks of dried fish slime covered his arms and shirt sleeves. He even smelled like a fish!

"Never mind," said Ma with a knowing smile. "It's a good thing it's Saturday. Go get some water and I'll get the tub ready for baths."

"Ma, Erik's pa just finished their sauna and he wondered if Pa and I could go try it tonight. Says they don't take baths in Finland—they just sweat the dirt out."

"Oh they do, do they?" said Ma, her hands on her hips.

Paul smiled. "Can I? Please?"

Ma nodded with a smile. "The girls will still need a bath."

He grabbed two buckets that sat by the door of the tent and headed for the pump. "I'll try to find them while I'm down that way."

"That's my boy." She smiled affectionately as she watched him walk down the hill with a happy skip, swinging the buckets. Then she turned back to the letter she'd been writing about how much she hated Alaska and ripped it up.

From a distance Paul made out the familiar sound of one of his ma's favorite songs coming from their piano. Paul stopped to look back toward the tent.

Well, what do ya know? Maybe Ma's getting used to things around here. He continued down the path, whistling along to Ma's tune. *What a day! Bears, eagles, loons, mountains, and great fishin'! This is the life!*

Chapter 17
The Sauna

Paul and Erik leaned against a tree and watched from a distance as men arrived on foot or in horse-drawn wagons. They congregated by the new sauna, talking, laughing, and smoking pipes, while Erik's two older brothers stoked the fire.

"That was a great fishin' hole. How'd you discover it?" Paul asked. "Or is that a secret, too?"

"Naw. I ran into a Native fella from Eklutna one day while I was explorin'. He said his people had been coming out there to fish for generations. He liked that spot because it was quiet and full of fish."

"He's sure right about that. The bear knew that, too!"

They both laughed.

"So, how does this sauna thing work?" asked Paul.

"Well, it's tradition, you know," said Erik. "First, they stoke the fire till it's almost unbearable in there. The men go in first, while the fire's the hottest. It's kind of a test to see how hot and how long you can handle it. After they come out, the younger boys go in and finally the women and little kids. Once we get the house built the women and kids will come over, too, and there'll be feasting like you wouldn't believe!"

"And you do this instead of takin' a bath in a tub?"

"Yep. Can't remember the last time I've had a bath—maybe never. This is how they've done it in Finland for centuries!" He looked at Paul. "You're not thinkin' of chickenin' out now, are you?"

"The thought had crossed my mind," Paul grinned. "Anybody ever die from this?"

"Not that I know of," Erik laughed. "In the wintertime they even run out and dive into snow or a lake afterwards."

"Well, if no one's ever died I guess I'll give it a try. Ma would be pretty upset if I died takin' a bath!"

Just then each of the men cut some small branches off a nearby tree and entered the room attached to the sauna.

"What are the branches for?"

"Oh, you'll find out," smiled Erik with his devilish grin. "And we'll see just how tough you are, too."

"I don't think I like the sound of that!"

An hour later the men finished.

"Your turn, Paul," grinned Paul's Pa as he held the door open on his way out.

Paul, Erik, and two older boys stepped into the changing room. The others quickly undressed and went through the door into the sauna.

"Well, you comin'?" asked Erik.

"In a minute," mumbled Paul.

Erik seemed to read Paul's mind. "In Finland, if you're gonna be a man, you got to learn how to take a sauna!"

Two minutes later Paul opened the door and was hit with a blast of heat that seemed to burn his lungs when he breathed.

"This is like walking into a furnace!" he choked.

The three others grinned. This was going to be fun.

"The real test," said Erik matter-of-factly, "is to eventually sit on the upper benches—you know, where most of the heat is, for the longest. Where are the branches, Henry?"

"Right here."

"Good, we'll need those pretty soon."

Erik poured cold water on the rocks on top of the stove. Steam filled the sauna as they sat silently and let the heaviness of the heat soak into their bodies. Sweat began to trickle down Paul's face.

This sure feels good after a hard day of fishing and hauling water. I feel like I'm in a trance, he sighed.

Eddie, one of the older boys, took a rag from one of two buckets by the stove and began scrubbing himself. After he washed his hair with the soap, he took the other bucket and poured the whole thing over his head.

"Ah, that feels better. Be right back." He came in with another bucket of clean, cold water for the next person. One by one each washed himself and rinsed.

When Paul finished he closed his eyes and took a deep breath. Suddenly he heard a sharp slapping sound. Eddie was hitting Henry's back briskly with one of the branches until sweat poured out of him.

"Your turn," Erik grinned as he motioned for Paul to turn so he could smack his back.

It stung like hot tiny needles, but Paul wasn't about to complain. After a few minutes, he was drenched in sweat and almost felt sick.

"Okay," said Erik as he handed the branch to Paul. "Have at it."

Paul hit Erik's back over and over until it turned bright red and glistened with sweat.

"Good enough?" asked Paul, who was feeling rather weak and light-headed from the heat.

"Good enough," Erik winked at the other boys. "Think I'll sit up higher. It's not quite hot enough down low."

"Me, too," said both other boys as they climbed to the top bench.

Paul could barely stand the heat down low, but …*I can't give up now. If they can do it, I can do it.*

"How long we been in here?" Paul asked weakly a few minutes later.

"Oh, I reckon 'bout twenty minutes," said Eddie, the other boy.

"Dang, it seems a lot longer than that!" Paul breathed heavily. "Don't think I feel too good." He moved back down to the lower bench and held his head in his hands. "How do men last a whole hour?"

Ten minutes later Paul could barely stand as he nearly fell out the sauna door. He gasped for air and, wrapped in a towel, collapsed on the floor of the changing room. He could vaguely hear the other boys howling with laughter.

Maybe a plain ol' bath in Ma's metal tub ain't so bad after all! he decided.

Chapter 18
Airplanes

Long days of summer passed. As August came the mosquitoes dwindled only to be replaced by little gnats called no-see-ums. Their bite was almost worse than mosquito's. Wild berries grew everywhere. Cranberries, currants, raspberries, and blueberries kept families busy filling buckets.

"Goodness, look at this big patch!" exclaimed Maggie's mother. "It's so wonderful finding berries right here on our very own land!"

"I know. I found a big one over here!"

Maggie and her mother picked cranberries as fast as they could, each quiet in their own thoughts. Though there was coolness to the air, the sun was warm on their backs.

"At least it's not as tempting to eat these like it is blueberries!" Maggie scrunched up her face as she tried one.

"They are pretty tart, aren't they?" laughed Mother. "I heard there's a good recipe for cranberry ice cream."

"Yuck! That sounds terrible"

"Well I just might try it," smiled Mother. "Ready for some lunch?"

"Yes, I'm starving!"

They spread out one of the gray wool blankets from the tent and enjoyed leftovers from last night's supper.

"I love the view of the mountains," sighed Maggie.

"Yes, we were lucky to get this homesite, weren't we?" Ma nodded. "I have a treat for dessert," she winked.

"Is it cake?"

"No, it's better—at least better for you!" Mother brought out two large oranges from the basket.

"Oh!" Maggie eagerly grabbed one. "I love oranges and we hardly ever get them."

"Fresh fruit, at least edible fresh fruit, is pretty hard to come by up here, isn't it?"

"This orange reminds me of the time Francine, Paul, and I climbed the Butte." She pointed to the tall hill that stood alone on the other side of the Matanuska River. You could see the Butte, which the area was named for, from all over the big valley.

"It was a really hot day and it seemed like we hiked straight up, though it's not nearly as high as the mountains around here. Still, by the time we got to the top we were hungry and thirsty and full of scratches. When you get near the top it's almost straight up! My knees were bruised and bleeding where I fell on some rocks." Maggie took a bite of her biscuit and went on.

"When we finally stood on the top it was like being on top of the world! You could see so far in every direction! Do you know what we saw up there?"

"No, what?"

"A red airplane! It was actually below us, and when it flew next to the mountains it looked so tiny you could hardly see it!"

"That's amazing."

"But the best part," continued Maggie as she peeled her orange, "was when we sat down and watched that little red airplane and ate oranges that Francine's mom had given us. They were so sweet and juicy! Mmm, that was the first orange I had eaten since Seattle."

"I believe you're right. And speaking of Francine, her mother gave me these oranges! They went into Anchorage the other day and were kind enough to bring us some."

"That was nice." Maggie bit into a section of orange and juice ran down her chin.

"Maggie, speaking of airplanes, do you remember me telling you about how an airplane landed in Saindon's field a few days ago? The one with two famous men in it—Will Rogers and Wiley Post?"

Maggie nodded.

"Mr. Rogers was so impressed with the colonists and wanted to see an actual colony home. I heard he gave candy to the children that came out to see them in the field. Wish we'd known about it." She paused in thought.

"Well, the sad truth is, their plane crashed the next day near Barrow, way up in northern Alaska, and they both died."

"Really? Died?"

Maggie sat looking around at the mountains that surrounded them, deep in thought while she ate the rest of her orange.

"Do you think women could fly airplanes?"

"Well, dear, I don't see why not!"

"I know it's dangerous, Mother," she turned and said very seriously. "I know planes can crash and all, but I decided something that day we were up on the Butte."

"I'm afraid to ask."

"Someday I want to fly an airplane!"

"Maggie May, I declare! You never fail to amaze me!"

Chapter 19
Termination Dust

"Termination dust, what's that?" asked Maggie as she and Paul stood outside the Palmer post office with their new friend, Sam.

"It's the first snow up there on Pioneer Peak," Sam pointed. "And it means summer is pretty much over."

They both looked up at the mountain that majestically stood guard over the Matanuska Valley. It looked like the peak had been dusted with powdered sugar.

"Ugh!" Maggie groaned. "How can summer be over? It's only August!"

"Such is life in the far north," Sam shrugged. "You'll get used to it."

They had met Sam while walking to town a few weeks earlier. His mother was D'naina Indian and his father was white. The family lived on a homestead north of town and were well known for their kindness and growing potatoes. Sam, one of eight children, was Maggie's age, and they became friends right away.

"Hey, did you see the new school buses that came on the train yesterday?" groaned Maggie. "I was hoping they'd forget about sending us to school way up here in Alaska!"

"Ha! They thought of everything—well, not according to some people, but just about everything!" laughed Paul.

"Where do you go to school?" Maggie asked Sam.

"I guess we'll have teachers come to our house again." He looked toward the new school building that transient workers were busy building. "But that's where we'll all be going once they get it done. How about you?"

"A teacher stopped by Camp 8 the other day and said we'll be going to Matanuska," Paul sighed as he kicked a small rock. "I'm not too excited, to be honest."

"It won't be so bad. At least the school building will be warmer than your tent!" he smiled. "How much longer you all going to live in them things anyway? It gets pretty windy and cold come winter."

"Yeah, I've heard! Father says the house is coming along but they have to keep waiting for supplies from Seattle." Maggie shrugged her shoulders.

"Ours is getting there, too," said Paul. "Pa's at the doc's in Anchorage right now getting his cast off, so it'll probably start goin' faster. Been lots of delays, that's for sure."

"Well, my Pa says that's the government for you. Too much red tape, whatever that means." Sam slung his bag of potatoes over his shoulder. "I got to keep going. Ma will be mad if I'm not home soon."

"Mine, too! And I'm sorry I can't buy any potatoes from you. I had to buy these with credit." Maggie held up her bag of potatoes from the commissary.

"That's okay. Thanks anyway. See ya."

They waved as Maggie and Paul headed into the post office and Sam headed north for home.

"Wish I could have bought potatoes from him. It's silly we can only buy food at the commissary."

"Yeah, it doesn't make a whole lot of sense," Paul glanced at Maggie as the postmaster handed him a handful of letters and a catalog.

Both eagerly looked through their mail. It was always exciting to see if anyone had written from back home.

"Oh look," said Maggie. "Here's a letter from the Hansons who moved back Outside. Heard they ended up in Seattle, since that's as far as the government would pay their way. I wonder how big baby Joey is getting."

Paul was engrossed in the thick Montgomery Ward's catalog that had finally come. "Ma was sure hopin' this would be here. She is chompin' at the bit to order our furniture."

"Yeah, our catalog came yesterday and I don't think Mother's hardly said two words. She must have every page memorized by now! Says it'll be like Christmas to have the house done and new furniture to put in it."

"May I be a gentleman?" Paul smiled as he carried her groceries back to camp.

"Then I'll be a lady and carry your mail," she replied slyly.

"You just want to look through the catalog!" he laughed.

"Maybe," she grinned, as she leafed through the pages while they walked along the dirt road.

"That's what they're wearing now?" she said out loud as she studied the styles in the girls' section. "Oh, I love that one! That would be perfect for the dance."

"The Harvest Dance?" he asked.

"Yeah," Maggie smiled, and was suddenly embarrassed to have brought up the dance.

"I didn't think you liked wearing dresses," he teased.

"Well, I guess I am sort of a tomboy, but I like wearing a dress now and then," she tried to sound somewhat feminine.

Paul was silent for a moment, then took a breath and blurted out, "Would you like to go to the dance with me? That is, if you want to. You don't have to if you don't want. I know it's not for another month, but …"

Maggie smiled at Paul's awkwardness, and put her finger up to her head as if she needed to think about it first.

"Well, yes, I'd like that," she finally said.

They both walked on in an uncomfortable silence. Neither one knew what to say. Paul started to whistle until they reached Maggie's tent.

"Hi there, David. Here you go." He tried to sound nonchalant as he laid the groceries on the table.

"Thanks, Paul," answered David.

"Here's your mail," Maggie blushed as she handed him the mail and their eyes met.

"See you all later," Paul said quickly, and off he went down the row of tents, whistling merrily.

David looked at Maggie. "Do I sense a little something different?"

"What? I have no idea what you're talking about!" declared Maggie, blushing again.

"Hmmm. Just wondered. Must be my imagination," he smiled as he turned to leave. "Better go get some kerosene for the lamps before

Mother gets back or she'll tan my hide." He winked at Maggie as he stepped outside the tent.

"Oh!" Maggie put her hands on her hips and stomped her foot just as Mother came in the door.

"Goodness, what's gotten into you?"

"Brothers, that's what." Her voice softened. "But now that you're here I was wondering if there would be any way to order a little something from the catalog?"

"Well, there's not a lot of extra money. But what might that be?" Mother was curious.

"Let me get it and I'll show you."

Meanwhile, back at Paul's tent, Ma had her head out the door waiting for Paul. "So, did it come? Oh, thank goodness! I can't wait to look at the furniture! Oh, to have a hot cup of tea and look through my Montgomery Ward's catalog. What more could a woman want?" She almost grabbed the catalog from Paul's hands.

"Well," said Pa, who had recently returned from seeing the doctor in Anchorage. "I'd think a nice warm house instead of the drafty little tent might be kinda nice."

"Oh," answered Mother half listening as she flipped through the pages. "I don't mind the tent so much. It's been a great adventure— something to tell my grandkids about."

Paul suddenly looked up at Pa and realized he was back from the doctor. "You got your cast off! How does your arm feel?"

"It's pretty weak, I have to admit. Pretty stiff, too." He winced as he tried to bend his arm at the elbow. "Doc says it'll be back to normal before too long."

"Things do seem to work out, just like Helen always says," Ma muttered. "Better get my furniture ordered. I hear it takes months to get here!" Ma hummed happily as she sat looking through the pages.

"Come on, girls," Paul shuffled Minnie and Clara out of the tent. "Better leave Ma alone for a while."

As everyone prepared for bed, Paul walked sleepily down the path to the water pump. He shivered. There was definitely a chill in the air. Looking up at Pioneer Peak he shivered again. More termination dust.

Chapter 20
School

A few days later Ma woke Paul and the girls up bright and early. "Time for your first day of school in Alaska!" she sang cheerfully. "The bus will be here in half an hour. And your oatmeal is ready."

"Ugh!" They pulled the covers over their head. Neither Ma's oatmeal nor school ranked as favorites.

"You ready for sixth grade?" Paul smiled at Maggie as he and Erik sat down in the bus seat behind her.

"Guess I'll have to be. How about you?" she said sleepily.

"I am! Well, I mean I'm ready for seventh. Already did sixth!" Erik was his usual enthusiastic self. "At least Matanuska has a real school. I haven't been there since our belongings came back in June. Remember trying to get your ma's piano onto that wagon and up the hill? Poor horses!"

"Boy, do I! My back hurts thinkin' about it!" groaned Paul. "Did ya hear that the little kids at main camp are going to school in that boxcar by the tracks?"

"That would be kind of fun!" said Maggie. "Imagine that!"

They all laughed.

"Francine said they made the community hall into a school in the Butte but everyone has to walk every day," continued Maggie.

"Brrrr. That'll be cold in the winter," shivered Erik. "See how lucky we are to have a bus?"

"Wish I could be in Sam's shoes," murmured Paul as he looked out the window. "The teacher comes to the house once a week. Soon as she'd leave I'd be out the door to go fishin' or somethin'. Can't stand the thought of bein' inside all day." He sighed heavily.

"Yeah," Maggie looked at him knowingly. "It'll about kill you."

"It'll kill me for sure," Paul smiled. "This has been the best summer anyone could dream up! Hikin', explorin', fishin' every day! Sure hate to see it end."

The bus stopped in front of a square, two-story building on the main street of the little boardwalk town of Matanuska, five miles back toward Anchorage. Before Palmer, Matanuska had been the main train depot for the local settlers and homesteaders in the area. The colonists' household goods were picked up there and brought to tent city by horse and wagon.

"I hear the mighty Matanuska River floods every now and then, and the town is pretty much under water. Maybe we'll be lucky and we won't have school for a while," said Paul hopefully.

"Too bad that's only in the spring when the ice goes out of Lake George, way up in the mountains," laughed Erik. "Say, an old-timer told me some of the icebergs that come down from the Knik Glacier are as big as a house!"

"That's hard to imagine!" Maggie was skeptical as they disembarked from the bus. "How do you seem to know so much about practically everything?"

"Got a nose for news, I guess!"

"Good morning, students. Welcome to Matanuska School," greeted Principal Anderson, a tall, middle-aged man. "All seventh-through twelfth-graders go around the corner, first- through sixth-graders go on upstairs."

"Well, I guess you're up with the little kids," teased Paul. "Have fun!"

As he and Erik disappeared around the corner, Paul glanced back at Maggie. She scrunched up her face and stuck out her tongue. "Come on Minnie and Clara," she said loud enough for Paul to hear. "I'll make sure you find your rooms."

The bus dropped everyone off at the edge of Camp 8 at the end of the day.

"How was your first day of school in Alaska?" asked Ma as Paul came through the tent door. She had a plate of cookies on the table.

"All I could think about was gettin' outta there. But it really wasn't that bad. Miss Adams is nice. Guess I'll live after all! Mmm, good cookies!"

Meanwhile, with winter fast approaching, the transient workers were furiously trying to finish building everything needed for a new town. Hammers and saws worked nonstop on the new hospital, new school, dorms for teachers, houses for ARRC employees, a new community center, churches, warehouses for food and dairy products, and, most importantly, colonists' houses. There was a lot to do in a short amount of time.

"Have you noticed how the days are getting shorter?" Pa stated a couple of weeks later.

"I get up every mornin' and look at how far the snow has moved down Pioneer Peak and it gets me moving!"

"Well, I'm happy things are gettin' closer, but I miss bein' able to visit with the other womenfolk like before we moved to the homesite," Ma sighed. "It made life a little easier."

"But it's also easier to work on the house now that we've moved the tent right next to it," Pa reminded her. "We'll see everyone at the dance in a few days and catch up on things."

Paul shivered as he got out of his cot the next morning. He could see his breath. Ma was at the stove trying to get the fire going.

"The water froze in the teakettle last night," she grumbled. "How are we gonna keep from freezing? It's only the end of September!"

No matter how hard she tries, Ma still has a hard time gettin' used to life up here. Will Ma ever be happy in Alaska? Lots of others have already left.

"Here, Ma," said Paul patiently. "I'll get it going, don't worry."

Ma sat down on the bench and sighed. "Your Pa's been workin' on that house from dawn to dusk, but it seems like it'll never be done. I worry about his arm—it still hurts him. What if he gets hurt again liftin' those logs or somethin'? And this mornin' the clothes were frozen on the line, and now the water on the stove! I don't think people were meant to live in this country!"

Paul looked around for some kindling.

"On top of everything else, I got a letter from Gram. Gramps isn't doing well, and she thinks he might have had a heart attack. As long as it took for me to get this letter, he might have died already! What if I never see him again?" The tears finally poured down her face.

So that's what Ma's so upset about. He was glad he had the task of lighting the fire, because he didn't know what to say. He couldn't bear the thought of something happening to Gramps. But leaving was unthinkable. Despite the hardships, Alaska was already in his blood.

Soon there was a warm fire blazing in the stove.

"I'll get more water on my way back from checking on Fannie. Maybe a nice cup of tea will help you feel better."

"Yes, it would. I'll get the girls up for school in a minute."

When Paul returned Ma was pouring hot water into her cup.

"I'm gonna have to find something to do now that you're all away all day, or your Pa will put me to work buildin' a house!" Ma's voice was a little stronger.

"Maggie's ma gets together with a homemakers group. Maybe you should do that."

"I'm not really much into that, but it sure does get lonely." She sat quietly for a moment. "You know, I think I will stop over and visit Helen today."

The bus came earlier now. Ma walked out to the road with Paul, Minnie, and Clara. As they stood waiting, Paul noticed a movement down the road. Out stepped a bull moose with a huge set of antlers on his head, about fifty feet away. The moose noticed Paul's family at the same time and, with his long gangly legs, took off at a fast trot down the road in the opposite direction.

"Wow," whispered Paul. "That's the first moose I've seen. Must be tryin' to find food now that snow is movin' down the mountains."

"That was too close for comfort!" exclaimed Ma. "He's as big as a horse! What if he'd come this way?"

"He's more afraid of you than you of him," said Paul, trying to reassure her, though he was a little shaken as well.

"My heart's still beatin' fast!" Ma held her chest while the girls hid behind her.

"Well, it sure would be good to have some moose meat for the winter! I'll have to tell Pa and maybe we can scout around once huntin' season opens."

"I don't think they're lettin' us hunt until next year, though I heard a few fellas are goin' north up the road a ways and huntin' anyway. It would take me all winter to can that much meat! But, it would be nice havin' something besides fish." She smiled at Paul.

Ma waved as the bus drove away, then she started toward Helen's house.

"Helen, did you see that huge moose down the road?" she exclaimed as Helen invited her into her tent.

"Why, no! And you were brave enough to walk a quarter mile here knowin' it was out there somewhere?"

"Why, now that you mention it, I guess I was, wasn't I? Was I brave, or just crazy?"

They both laughed

"Mary, you are going to be one tough Alaskan woman yet, mark my words!"

Chapter 21
Maggie's Birthday

"Happy birthday, dear Maggie, happy birthday to you!" the family sang as Mother brought a cake with flaming candles to the table.

"How does it feel to be twelve?" she asked. "Amost a teenager."

"Well, I got teased all day at school, but other than that, not much is different," she smiled. "Do I look different?" She turned in a circle.

"Practically a grown woman!" teased Michael.

After they had finished eating cake Maggie opened her gifts. She got some stationery from David, a pretty blue ribbon for her hair from Michael, a book from Father, and a couple of cards from relatives in Michigan. One card even had a crisp dollar bill in it.

"That's worth a lot, especially down there," said Father.

She gave everyone a hug. "Thanks everyone. And don't worry, I'll send them a thank you note," she said before Mother reminded her.

"Wait a minute, there's one more for my favorite daughter!" Mother pulled a nicely wrapped box out from under a cot.

"You mean your only daughter!" Maggie laughed.

"Well, you're still my favorite!"

Maggie carefully unwrapped the pretty paper. She lifted the lid and caught her breath. It was the pretty dress she had wanted from the catalog.

"Mother, you ordered it! How could you afford it?" her eyes were wide with happiness.

"Well, I sold a few pies and cakes here and there and saved up. I'm glad you're happy." Mother kissed her on the forehead.

"And now, I have a surprise for all of you," said Father as he winked at Maggie. "Even Mother doesn't know about it."

They waited with eager anticipation to hear Father's news.

"We'll be ready to move into our new house sometime next week!" Everyone jumped up and clapped. Mother and Father did a do-si-do in the middle of the tent as they laughed and hugged each other.

"It has been a memorable four and a half months in our lovely little abode, but it's time we move out and Darlene moves in!"

"The cow is going to live in our tent?" exclaimed Maggie.

"Why not? She's getting kind of cold out there in her pen with no shelter," said David.

"Land sakes," said Mother. "If we can live all these months in a tent, I guess Darlene can, too!"

"Can the ducks come in, too?" asked Maggie.

"Whoever wants to move in is welcome," Father laughed. "But I'm going to need everyone's help to get the house done enough, though it won't be completely finished."

"I'll be happy no matter what," commented Mother. "It'll seem like a castle after living here!"

"Yes, well, castles can be cold, drafty places, you know. And I'm afraid that's how the house might be for a while," Father sighed as he sat down to rest.

Maggie reached down and put her arms around Father's neck. "You're the best father in the whole world, and I've had the happiest birthday ever!" She kissed him on the cheek with a noisy smack.

"Knock, knock," said a voice that sounded like Paul. He and Erik stood at the tent door. "We heard there might be a birthday going on over here."

"Come on in, boys," said Father. "We were just celebrating that and the news that we'll be moving into our house next week."

"That's exciting!" Paul smiled. "I think we'll be one of the last ones, which doesn't make Ma too happy."

"It'll be a while for us, too!" said Erik. "Did you hear my Pa made them tear the first house down and start over because they didn't build it right?"

"No, but I could see your father doing that," laughed Father. "Maybe I should have him come over and check mine out before we move in!"

"I would think about that first, Mr. Cooper." Erik laughed. "What you don't know might be okay!"

They all laughed as the boys sat down at the table.

"Have some cake," Mother handed them a plate.

"Mmmm. This is delicious!" both said between mouthfuls.

"I found a little something for you, Maggie." Paul took a small box out of his pocket and handed it to Maggie.

She opened the box to find a miniature red airplane.

"Paul, I love it! How did you remember? "

"You made such a fuss about the airplane that day on the Butte, it wasn't hard," he laughed.

"And I made a little something for you, too," Erik handed her a gift wrapped in brown paper.

Maggie noticed a funny expression on Paul's face out of the corner of her eye.

"A duck!" she exclaimed. "Did you whittle this?"

Erik laughed. "Well, you like ducks and I like to whittle! Most girls want girly things, like my sisters," Erik teased. "But not you!"

"Maybe we can all learn to fly together some day," Paul laughed, somewhat sarcastically.

"Thanks, guys," Maggie laughed and pretended not to notice as she flew the little airplane through the air. "There's never a dull moment with you two around!"

"Nope, never!" Paul seemed to be a hurry as he motioned for Erik to go. "See ya."

Maggie waved and watched them for a while until they disappeared into the dimness of the night.

As they walked down the road, Paul felt a strange emotion inside.

"What's the idea, tryin' to make me look stupid?" he suddenly blurted out as he elbowed Erik in the side.

"Ow! What d'ya mean?" Erik hadn't expected it.

"Yeah, like you don't know what I'm talkin' about!" He didn't know what this feeling was, but it made him feel angry.

Suddenly Paul swung around and slugged Erik. Erik's nose started bleeding, and he groaned as he held his face.

"What's gotten into you?" Blood spurted through Erik's fingers and down his hands.

He spit some out of his mouth and onto the road.

Paul stopped and took a deep breath.

"Hey, I'm sorry, pal. Here, hold this," he took a rag out of his pocket.

"Wow, I didn't see that comin'!" Erik shook his head and held the rag to his nose as they started down the road.

"I didn't either," Paul murmured. "Sorry."

They walked further, both silent.

"I think you're jealous!" Erik suddenly blurted out. "Yep, you're jealous that I gave Maggie a gift for her birthday, aren't ya?"

"Naw, I don't care—"

"Oh yes you do. I saw that look in your eyes when she opened mine."

"Well, maybe you're right. Sure didn't think it bothered me that much." Paul put his thumbs through his belt loops and walked with his head hung low.

"Hey, don't worry about it," Erik elbowed him back in the ribs.

"Ouch! Guess I deserved that," Paul grimaced, holding his side in pain.

"Yep. But don't worry, Maggie's not my type," he chuckled, still holding the rag to his nose. "She's way too stubborn and independent for me."

"You think?" Paul's face brightened.

"Yep. I want some gal that'll cook and clean and doesn't have any desire to fly red airplanes!"

They both laughed and pushed each other jokingly as they walked along.

"Oh, it hurts to laugh," Erik felt his face. "You didn't give me a black eye, did ya?"

"Um, well, sure looks like it might be." Paul inspected his eye carefully. "Kinda too dark out to tell."

"That's great. How am I gonna explain this?"

"Oh, you'll think of something. You better, cuz if you ever tell anyone, I'll have to do something worse!"

"You ever sock me again, I'll lock you in the sauna and let you melt to death!"

"Ha! Well, I believe ya, so I'll control myself next time," he laughed.
They walked on in silence for some time.

"Girls!" said Erik.

"Girls!" agreed Paul.

Back at Maggie's house she helped her mother finish up the dishes.

"Thanks for the best birthday ever!" she kissed her mother on the cheek, then yawned. "Think I'll go to bed now. I'm tired."

"Good night, dear."

She lay in bed, thinking, for quite a while, then opened her diary.

> Dear Diary,
>
> My first birthday in Alaska. Twelve sounds kind of old! It was a wonderful day, especially when Paul and Erik stopped by. He gave me a red airplane—can you believe it? Erik carved me a duck. Can't wait to go to the dance in my new dress! Had fun in school. Joined Four H Club with Francine, so at least I'll see her once in a while! Tired.
>
> Love, Maggie

Chapter 22
The Dance

It wasn't unusual for a truck of transient workers to drive past Maggie's tent to help with the new log home nearing completion.

"Hi, there! Working hard, I see!" Francine smiled as she peeked in the tent door.

Maggie looked up from scrubbing clothes on the washboard.

"Francine! What in the world are you doing over this way?" Maggie wiped her wet hands on her shirt and ran over to hug Francine, ducking to avoid wet clothes. Both laughed and screamed with joy. "Yes, I'm working hard and I've got the scars to prove it." She pretended to pout as she held up her two little fingers. Both were red and swollen from being rubbed raw on the washboard. "Our gasoline washing machine died the other day and Father hasn't had time to look at it. He works day and night on the house. Had forgotten how much I hated washing clothes by hand, especially when it's cold out!"

Water had spilled all over the table and was dripping into puddles on the floor. Clothes hung on lines stretched back and forth across the tent to dry with the heat of the crackling fire.

"Tell me about it! It never ends!" Francine sighed as she sat down at the table. "It's cozy in here. But I have to tell you the news! Did you hear Mother had her baby?"

"No! What did she have?"

"Dr. Albrecht just delivered my new little baby brother yesterday! I had to come tell you as soon as I could get away." Her face beamed with happiness.

"My, your tent is going to seem pretty small with six kids!"

"That's okay. One big happy family, you know! Should be moving into the house before long anyway."

"Us, too!" Maggie went back to work scrubbing her father's shirt. "How did you get here?"

"Oh, Reverend Bingle often brings a load of folks back when he visits someone out our way. Pa and I just had to see Mother and the baby. We don't have a name picked out yet, but he's so cute! We hitched a ride with the workers when we heard they were coming to your place. My pa's been anxious to see your father, too."

"We could see each other more often if it wasn't so scary crossing that river, don't you think? I bet we can get together all the time once it freezes up!"

"I sure hope so. Speaking of get-togethers, you are going to the dance tonight, aren't you?" Francine leaned forward with a hopeful look on her face.

"Wouldn't miss it! I got a new dress for my birthday just for the dance. Are you?"

"Yes! Actually, I wondered if I could get ready here and go with you?" She held up a bag of clothes. "Mother said I should go and take a break for a change. She'll be in the hospital for another day, and Pa said he'd stay home with the kids."

"Of course you can get ready here! That'll be so much fun! We can do each other's hair!"

Both girls giggled and caught up on news from school.

"There, the last shirt!" Maggie threw the dirty water outside. "It wouldn't be so bad if they didn't need to be ironed, too," she sighed. "I hate ironing!"

"I kinda like it. It's a nice time to think, and everything looks so crisp and nice when you're done."

"You are terribly responsible," Maggie shook her head. "Don't you know it makes the rest of us look bad? We better find you a suitable fella pretty soon—one that wants to settle down and all that."

"Well," Francine looked down at the floor and blushed. "To tell you the truth there is someone I was hoping to meet at the dance."

"Really? Who?"

"Andy Welsh. You remember him—he's from Wisconsin and his family got land in the Butte, too. They kept their tent in the main camp for a while like we did, but now that everyone's moved to their own places we don't see each other, except at school, of course."

"Isn't he a few years older?"

"Yeah, but that's not a big deal. I'm almost thirteen. And he has the most beautiful blue eyes …" Francine's words drifted into space as she sat daydreaming.

"Uh, oh. If I didn't know better, I'd say you're falling for him!"

Just then Francine's father poked his head in the tent to say he was heading back with the workers and to remind Francine to have fun. They waved goodbye from the tent door.

"Okay, now let me see that new dress," she said excitedly.

"Well, it needs to be ironed yet."

"Good! Let's heat your iron up. It'll be so pretty when I'm done!"

The afternoon was spent ironing clothes, and washing and curling each other's hair. Maggie wore the blue ribbon from David in her long brown hair. It matched her new dress perfectly. Francine's curly blond hair was tied up with a green bow to match her plaid skirt and sweater.

Before long the school bus honked as it came to a stop outside Maggie's tent. Like taxis, buses were used for events like dances, which were a highlight for the colonists.

Maggie's family and Francine joined the other families already on the bus, including Erik's and Paul's.

"Wow, is that you, Maggie?" Paul teased as she and Francine sat down in front of him and Erik. "You're actually wearing a dress? I never thought I'd see the day!"

"You two look beautiful!" Erik let out a low whistle.

"Why, thank you!" they giggled. They both carried coats since the weather was getting cold.

At the warehouse, the colony families filed off the bus in front of the warehouse, everyone all dressed up and chatting excitedly. It was important to visit, catch up on news, and have some much-needed fun.

Maggie, Francine, Paul, and Erik were the last to spill out of the bus, laughing and joking as they skipped up the steps to the warehouse.

"Look at this crowd. Must be because it's the Harvest Dance that everyone's here tonight," Paul observed. "Don't get lost," he smiled as he took Maggie's hand.

Maggie blushed but hung on tight as they wove their way through the crowd.

The warehouse had been cleaned up and cleared out. Bales of straw placed side by side along the far end of the room were for kids to sit and fall asleep on as the night grew late. The sound of the local band of colony musicians, mingled with voices and laughter, filled the air as men, women, children, and dogs filed in and out of the doors. Many of the men, including some officials from ARRC, stood along the walls, smiling as they watched the colonists enjoy themselves.

"Is that the dress from the catalog?" Paul asked when he took Maggie's coat. "It's way prettier on you!" He smiled approvingly.

"You were teasing me about it on the bus," Maggie's eyes sparkled with happiness.

"Well, I can't compliment you in front of Erik. I'd never live it down!"

"Well, I'll take it now then. Thank you!" Maggie curtsied and laughed. "Mother ordered it for my birthday."

Just then Erik and Francine walked up and the foursome wandered around the room, trying to find others they knew, and yelling to be heard over the music.

"Look, over there," Francine nudged Maggie's arm as she tilted her head over to a group of boys on one side of the room.

"Which one is Andy?"

"He's got curly brown hair and is wearing a plaid shirt. Come on, I'll introduce you!"

Before Maggie could answer Francine was leading her by the hand toward the group.

"Hi, Andy," Francine smiled. "This is Maggie, my best friend. You remember me telling you about her?"

Andy nodded toward Maggie. "Nice to meet you, Maggie."

"You do have pretty eyes!" Maggie blurted out. Francine gave her a sharp elbow to the ribs, which made Maggie catch her breath but she kept smiling. "Sorry, I mean, it's nice to meet you, too."

"I've seen you around camp. Quite a little baseball player, if I remember right," Andy laughed and the other boys joined him.

Maggie blushed, but before she had time to answer, she felt a tap on her shoulder.

"Wanna dance?" Paul asked with a serious look on his face.

"Do I have a choice?" Maggie giggled as she followed him toward the dance floor.

"Right now, no."

"But I was just meeting Francine's new friend," she had a confused look on her face.

"Yeah, I've heard about him. Rumor has it he and his buddies are behind some of the people's things that have gone missing 'round here lately."

"Then I need to warn Francine—"

"Not right now. Looks like they're busy."

Andy and Francine had joined the dance floor which was packed with parents, young people, and little kids all swaying to the music. A colonist from Minnesota played the fiddle, the Catholic priest was the drummer, and a married couple from Michigan played the guitar and saxophone. After playing a few songs, they stopped for a break.

"Come on, let's go get something to eat," Paul motioned to the table where popcorn and root beer sold for five cents.

Francine came up from behind and slipped her arm through Maggie's. "There you are!" She led Maggie outside. "At least we can hear each other talk out here!" she laughed. "So, what do you think?"

"About what?"

"You know, about Andy."

"Well, he seems nice. And I see what you mean about his eyes! But," Maggie hesitated, as if she had more to say.

"But, what?"

"Well, but he is older, and you just shouldn't get too serious," she blurted out.

"Oh, I'm not going to fall all head over heels for him. It's just kind of fun, you know, having someone notice you. You know—like Paul notices you."

"What? Francine McKenzie! We're nothing but friends! And it's going to stay that way!"

Francine sighed. "Yes, Maggie dear. Whatever you say. Come on, let's go back in and just have fun. I don't get many nights out!"

It was well after midnight when weary but happy parents gathered up their sleeping children from the bales of straw to board and head home. Fathers slung bigger kids over their shoulders while mothers carried little ones in their arms.

"Goodnight all," Francine waved as she boarded the bus back to the Butte. The others returned her wave.

"Look," said Maggie. "Francine's sitting with Andy on the bus. I knew I should have told her."

"Don't worry," said Paul. "I'm sure she'll figure things out."

"The nights are so dark now," whispered Maggie as they gazed up at the sky. "Don't the stars look like diamonds?"

"Yes, they sure do," Paul replied, but he was looking at Maggie, not at the stars.

She smiled, then gave him a little shove. "Don't look at me like that!" she giggled.

"Why not?"

"Because, we're just friends, right?"

"Right," Paul smiled.

They all headed to their bus. Paul sat beside her, though Erik sat behind them and kept them all entertained with jokes and observations of who was with who at the dance. Everyone laughed the entire way back.

Good nights were said. One by one families disembarked from the bus at their homesite and faded into the darkness.

Maggie waved goodbye to Paul as he got off before her. He smiled and waved back, then turned to walk with his parents and sisters down the moonlit trail to their tent.

Like fireflies back home, each tent came alive with a soft glow as kerosene lamps were lit. Dances were like family reunions, and in this land of extremes, far from family and loved ones, they helped keep the colony project alive.

Chapter 23
Winter Troubles

A few nights later Maggie was awakened by noises of the wind battering the tent. She sat up and rubbed her eyes. The tent would fill up with air, then heave from side to side as a gust slammed into it.

"Brrr," she rubbed her arms to warm up. "Is that you, Father?"

"It's me." He said quietly as he bent over the stove. "Having trouble keeping the stove lit. Every time I get the fire going again a gust comes down the stack and blows it out."

"What time is it?" she whispered. It was dark out and the others were still asleep.

"It's about three in the morning, and guess what it's doing outside."

Maggie crept to the door and peeked out. "It's snowing!" she shivered and jumped back under the covers.

"I'm afraid it's more like a blizzard," said Father. "Just hope the tent stays up for the night. Better check the stakes to be sure. And the animals."

He threw on his boots, coat, and hat. "Now where's that log splitter to pound the stakes with?" he muttered to himself.

"I think it's over by the woodpile," whispered Maggie.

"Right. Just hope I can find the woodpile," he winked.

Maggie fell in and out of sleep. She didn't hear the loud crash from outside. Some time later she sat up suddenly and looked around for Father.

"Mother, Michael, David!" she shook her brothers awake. "You've got to get up! I think something happened to Father!"

By now everyone was awake with alarm.

"Boys, get your things on. Oh my, listen to that wind! How long have you been awake, Maggie?"

"Off and on since three," Maggie said worriedly. "Father was trying to get the fire relit and went out to find the splitter to pound the tent stakes with. He was going to check the animals, too."

"Mercy," said Mother. "That was a while ago. Hurry boys. Here's a lantern. Is that snow?" she said as she opened the tent door. A big gust of wind blew snowflakes into the tent. "It's finally here. Do hurry, boys!"

She went to the stove to put more wood onto the coals. "The water's frozen in the kettle, too," she mumbled.

Maggie cracked the door to try to follow the faint glow of the lantern but the whipping snow swallowed it up into darkness. An occasional muffled yell of the boys calling for Father swirled on the wind back toward the tent. She closed the door and shuffled to the stove, wrapped in a blanket, to huddle by the struggling fire.

Minutes passed, but it seemed like an eternity.

Mother stayed busy thawing water and tending the fire. She put some mugs out for hot drinks when they all came back in.

"What if something terrible has happened to Father?" Maggie looked at Mother.

"The good Lord has helped us through many times before. He'll help us through this."

Michael and David had stepped into pelting snow that stung their faces like needles. They bent their heads into the wind to look for Father's tracks but blowing snow had covered them. There was no sign of him by the woodpile, and the splitter was still leaning against the stump.

"Father! Father!" they called over and over.

"Better go look by the animals," David hollered over the howling wind.

As they neared the cow's pen they could see that a tree had blown down across the path. Was that a dark form that lay under it?

"Father! Are you okay? Can you hear me?" called Michael as he ran up to the tree and knelt beside the still body. "Father, please answer me!"

Father moved one hand to tell them he was alive. His lips were blue. He tried to open his mouth to talk but no words came out.

"I think we can lift this limb enough to get him out," yelled David. "Quick, on the count of three. One, two, three!"

The boys strained to lift and move the tree a few inches.

"Again!" yelled Michael. "One, two, three!"

Another few inches were enough to free Father's legs.

"Come on, let's carry him back to the tent. We have to hurry!" Michael's voice was desperate.

Father screamed in pain as they lifted him from the ground.

Maggie had been watching for them out the tent door. "They found him!" she cried, as she opened the door and they literally blew in with the wind and snow.

Mother had moved a cot by the fire, and immediately wrapped Father with a blanket. As they helped him lie down he screamed again and grabbed his leg.

"Let me see that," said Mother as she gently removed his boots. "Is it this leg that hurts?" He nodded with a grimace as she rolled up his pant leg.

Maggie caught her breath when she saw a large area on his shin that was swollen and deformed. Once his socks were off they could see that his toes on both feet were white.

"I think his leg is broken," murmured Michael sympathetically. "That must hurt."

"Is that what frostbite looks like, Mother?" asked David, pointing to Father's toes.

Father shivered violently and moaned in pain.

"I've never seen frostbite, but I bet that's what it is. I think he came close to freezing to death! We have to get him warmed up!"

They tended to him all through the night. In the morning light the boys braved the storm to take care of the animals and bring in more wood. By afternoon things had calmed, and Michael started the three-mile hike to town to find Dr. Albrecht.

"My, my," the doctor said when they both returned in the early evening. He examined Father's leg and toes carefully. "Sure sounds like you're lucky to be alive," he looked up over his glasses at Father, then over to Mother.

Mother gave him a cup of coffee as he sat down at the table. He looked tired, as though he had been up all night.

"I'm pretty sure it's broken, but can't tell without an X-ray. It'll heal fine. Not sure about the toes, though. Frostbite and hypothermia are very dangerous conditions up here in the north. Time will tell."

"So I'll be laid up for a while, Doc?"

"Afraid so, Mr. Cooper. I'll need to X-ray and cast that leg in a couple of days, but you'll have to stay off your feet for a while with the frostbite."

"But—" Father started to protest.

"Or I'll admit you to the hospital where you won't have a choice," interrupted Dr. Albrecht.

"Don't that beat all?" sighed Father. "We were just ready to move into the house as soon as I got a couple of things done."

"Well, don't you worry too much about it. I'll see what I can do. In the meantime, here's some medicine for the pain. Max or myself will be back Thursday morning to pick you up. Good day." He finished his last swallow of coffee, nodded a thank you to Mother, grabbed his little black bag, and went out the door.

"Thank you, Doctor!" they all called.

Dr. Albrecht managed to get the word out alright. Bright and early two mornings later, Henry, Mr. Engles, Erik's Pa, and several transient workers arrived at the tent door, ready to work on the house. By midafternoon Mr. Engles came into the tent.

"Mrs. Cooper, we need you to let the fire die out so we can move the stove into the house. It might get a little chilly in here."

"Really? So soon?" Mother was surprised.

"Really," said Mr. Engles with a smile as he went back to the house.

"Good thing I made a big pot of chicken and dumplings a little early," said Mother. "They're going to be hungry!"

Two hours later the men entered the tent and removed everything but the stove and chair Father was sitting in.

"I declare," exclaimed Mother. "What wonderful friends we have!"

"Well, you'd better get over there and make sure they put things where you want them," said Father with a twinkle in his eyes. "You know how particular you are about that!"

"Yes, I hadn't thought of that. Don't worry, I'll make sure they don't forget you!" she smiled as she hurried out the door.

"Time for dinner!" announced David and Michael as they bounded into the tent a while later. Without hesitating, they picked up the chair with father in it and carried him into the new house.

"For he's a jolly good fellow, for he's a jolly good fellow, for he's a jolly good fellow, that nobody can deny," they all sang loudly as they carried him into the new living room and gently set his chair down.

He looked around. Though they still didn't have their furniture from Montgomery Ward's, Mother had unpacked some of her pictures and a few little things from back home. After all their work clearing and building, they were finally in their new home. He tried to say a few words but got choked up.

"We'll bring the other stove for the kitchen in after it cools down," said Erik's pa, filling the uncomfortable silence. "This one in the living room should keep you warm for a while."

"And there's still some insulation to put on the walls upstairs, so it'll be a mite chilly till then," added Henry.

"We'll help get that done," said Michael. "We sure are thankful for all your help today."

"Well," said Mr. Engles. "We've all helped each other from day one and that's how it has to be if we're going to make it up here."

"Amen to that!" said Mother, setting the table. "We don't have much for furniture, but please help yourself to some supper, gentlemen."

Maggie had a hard time falling asleep that night. She wrote in her diary:

> Oct. 10, 1935
> First night in our new house. Strange. Kind of lonely having my own room after so long all together in the tent. Mother is so happy, though Father was right, it is pretty cold and drafty. After nearly five months in a tent we have a real HOME! Thank you, God, for taking care of Father. Good night.
> Love, Maggie

Three days later Max stopped by to pick up Mother and Father. A few hours later Father hobbled into the house on crutches, his entire right leg in a cast.

"Still have to lie low for a few days till these toes heal, but after that, look out!" he chuckled. "These crutches are going to cover some territory!"

"What did Dr. Albrecht say about your toes?" asked Maggie.

"You all did such a good job nursing me back to health, he thinks they'll be fine. I'll have to be careful not to freeze them again, though."

"I'm going to knit you some thick wool socks to wear!" Mother bent down to kiss his cheek. "I think you're well on your way to being a real Alaskan sourdough!"

"Well thank you! I'll take that as a compliment!" Father laughed.

Chapter 24
Thanksgiving Reunion

Thanksgiving morning found colony women busy preparing food.

"Now, where did I put that bowl?" Paul heard Ma mumble to herself as he came through the back door with another load of wood. "As much as I love my new kitchen, I can't seem to find a thing." She opened another cabinet door. "Ah, there it is. Paul, can you get that down for me? Thanks, dear."

"When are the Ericksons picking us up, Ma?" he asked as he easily reached the upper shelf and handed her the bowl.

"Land sakes, look how tall you're getting!" She stepped back to look Paul up and down. "We've been so busy all this time I haven't noticed how you've grown like a weed! I'd say you need a haircut, too." She tousled his hair.

Paul's curly blond hair stuck out every which way from under his cap. He looked down at his dungarees which were up past his ankles, and his shoes were coming apart at the seams.

"Your shoes a bit too small?" she asked.

"Yeah, my toes've been pretty cramped for a while," he said, feeling a little embarrassed.

"A little! And you never once complained. They must be two sizes too small! Poor boy, we need to get you some new clothes as soon as we can." She turned to check the pies and put more wood in the stove. "Perhaps you and I could go into Anchorage with Maggie's folks when her pa gets his cast off in a couple of weeks."

"Boy, he'll be happy to have that off. Can't they do it out here? I hear they just finished the new hospital and it's pretty nice."

"That would be easier—I hadn't thought of that. We'll have to see," Ma was preoccupied looking for something else in the cupboard.

"So, when did you say the Ericksons are coming?" Paul asked again.

"They're supposed to be here around one. It'll be so nice to see everyone from Carlton County again! I hope my pies are done in time."

"They sure smell good!"

"Yes, they sure do," she smiled. "But you can't have any yet."

"Dang!" he snapped his fingers. "Say," he said, changing the subject. "Erik heard all the colonists were in their homes now. Is that true?"

"I heard the last family just moved into theirs a few days ago. Course, none of them are completely done, but glad we didn't have to wait that long. Brrrr!" Ma shuddered. "If it hadn't been for all the help we got, things would have been different."

"But Doc Albrecht and his new wife still live in a tent, don't they?"

"Now that you mention it they do. I don't think they'll be into a house any time soon, either. That's really roughing it, isn't it? Speaking of roughing it, could you fetch me more water?" She smiled and handed him a bucket.

"I don't know if I can do it, I have to walk so far!" he joked.

"Yes, it's awful having the pumphouse right in our yard," Ma laughed. "Imagine all the water you've hauled since we first landed in Palmer!"

"Between tent city and Camp 8, I've sure put in some miles! At least I don't have to wear that heavy wooden yoke anymore. I felt like an animal!" Paul exclaimed as he put on his coat. "Still, it feels like I pump water all day between watering Belle and the animals, not to mention us!"

Belle, who was never far from Paul's feet, looked up when she heard her name. Paul stroked her head.

"Like I've said before, don't know what I'd do without ya, son," Ma gave him a pat on the shoulder.

Paul walked out to the pumphouse with Belle running and jumping alongside him. Cold, clear water splashed into the bucket with each squeak of the pump handle.

There hadn't been any snow since the brief blizzard a few weeks before, and the constant winds had blown all that away. With the leaves off the birch, aspen, and cottonwood trees, the long, dark days of winter seemed dreary.

He smiled as he thought back on summer days of fishing and exploring with friends.

I wonder what Maggie's family's doing for Thanksgiving. Haven't seen her for nearly a week. He smiled again until the bucket overflowed and he felt freezing cold water seep into a hole in one of his shoes. *Serves me right—thinkin' of girls!*

The Ericksons were late arriving with their horse-drawn wagon, and by the time they got to the Engleses', the other five families from Carlton County, Minnesota were already there. The little house seemed to burst at the seams with people, laughter, and food. Their furniture had just arrived in time and all the women were admiring and comparing the furnishings.

A long table made with planks of wood sagged under the weight of bowls and platters of meats, breads, pies, and cakes. As the last dish was put out, Mr. Engles called everyone together. Youngsters tumbled down the stairs, and everyone stood side by side as he said grace.

"Dear Lord, we humbly gather together to thank you for your many blessings. A year ago none of us would have dreamed we'd be standing here in this house in the Matanuska Valley in Alaska. You have seen us through many adventures and challenges. And though things have sometimes been difficult, we have never gone hungry or not had a roof over our heads, even if it was made of canvas."

Everyone chuckled softly.

"We thank you for our families," he continued. "For our homes, and most of all for our friends. Be with our loved ones back home, and give us the strength to continue on through the winter months ahead. Bless this food! Amen!"

Everyone said "Amen!" They feasted, caught up on news, sang to guitars, and danced to fiddles until everyone's sides hurt from too much laughter, food, and fun, which continued well into the night.

Paul's family finally climbed into the wagon as the last of the families departed.

"Look!" Minnie pointed up at the nighttime sky.

Iridescent green, yellow, and pink ribbons flowed and undulated in the midnight darkness. They had seen the northern lights before, but never like tonight.

Oohs and aahs were heard all the way home as the aurora shone and danced in all its glory.

Paul felt a shiver go down his spine. *Life is never boring here! Just when you think you have Mother Nature all figured out, she surprises you with something new. I could never go back to Minnesota!*

Chapter 25
Tragedy

"Henry! Henry, you there?" A man banged on the front door until it seemed the glass would break.

Ma hurried to the door. "Hello, Mr. Williams. What can I do for you?"

"It's the Webber place outside of town. There's been an explosion and we need all the menfolk around to get over there. Don't look good."

"Henry's out back but I'll have Paul fetch him right away."

By the time Pa and Paul arrived at the Webbers' house it was burnt to the ground. Smoke rose from the pile of ashes and sections of the collapsed house, though in the dimness of the short December day it was hard to see details. Paul noticed a group of men huddled off to the side. One of them motioned to Pa.

"A real tragedy, Henry," he said, shaking his head.

"What happened?"

"Mr. Webber claims he accidentally put gasoline in the stove thinking it was kerosene. The whole place exploded."

"Anybody hurt?" Pa asked.

"Mrs. Webber had been standin' right next to the stove when it went off. She's at the hospital—burned real bad. Mr. Webber has some minor burns."

"What about the children?"

"Little girl was burned pretty bad, too. The older two weren't as serious."

"Terrible," Pa's eyes looked sad. "Anything we can do?"

"Nope, don't think so. House is a total loss. Mr. Webber will be at the hospital for a while, I reckon. His two brothers were both here for a visit." The man looked around. "Somebody'll need to check on the animals—"

"I'll take care of the animals," said Paul. *I'd rather do something than just stand here.*

Pa handed him the kerosene lamp. By now it was early evening and, without snow on the ground, it was dark. He headed out to the makeshift shed that many colonists had put up until their barns could be built next year. Lifting the lamp high he could make out a pig, a calf, and two cows. Everyone knew the Webbers had been selling milk to save for a trip back to Minnesota next summer. Paul felt a heavy sadness as he gave them all water, feed, and extra hay.

Memories of his house burning down in Minnesota, with the sounds and smells, made him feel sick. *How easily we could have died.*

"There, there, girl," he reassured one of the cows and patted her neck. "Unbelievable. They finally finish their house, are working so hard to go visit family, and something like this happens." He shook his head. "But I'll take care of ya, don't worry. I'll be back tomorrow to check on things."

News spread that Mrs. Webber died at the hospital the next day.

Three days later Erik stopped by to see Paul, who grabbed his coat and boots as they went out to sit out on the porch. Both were quiet for a few moments. Paul knew Erik had something to tell him.

"You hear about the Webbers' little girl?" Erik finally said.

"No, what?" Paul was afraid to ask.

"She died last night." He looked down at the stick he was whittling with his pocket knife. "She was only two." Tears welled up in his eyes, which was rare for Erik.

They both sat in silence. Paul looked out over the frozen landscape, dull, brown, and lifeless without snow. Scrubby-looking black spruce trees stood weakly next to skeletons of leafless trees and willow bushes. There was no wind for a change, and you could tell where neighbors' houses were by wisps of gray smoke that rose straight up from their chimneys.

Pioneer Peak and its fellow mountains loomed cold and silent across the river, seemingly undaunted by the trials of these new pioneers who had come to carve out a life in the north country. Perhaps they stood and watched those trials, wondering if steadfast perseverance and hard work would eventually win. Did they know there was to be a terrible price?

That people would be hurt, and some even die? Did they guess that many would give up and leave?

But the massive mountains that stood guard over this great valley had also persevered. Hadn't the fine silt that made the soil so fertile come from these very mountains that had been ground and pulverized by glaciers? Hadn't the trees that were weather-beaten and bent survived the hurricane-force winds that whipped down those glaciers and onto the plain time after time? Hadn't the Native Alaskans, who had been here for generations before the colonists had even heard about this land, found ways to survive the harsh, unforgiving climate and enjoy the bounty that it also provided?

Something stirred inside Paul as he sat there. Out of the grief of death came a resolve and a hope. He couldn't explain it, nor really understand it. All he knew was that he felt a bond with the mountains, and the trees, and the land. He felt a determination. Regardless of what might lie ahead, he knew inside that this was where he was meant to be. He knew that life here would have a different meaning than it had in Minnesota, a different purpose born out of the challenge of survival. He looked over at Erik and wondered if he felt the same way. It was too personal to talk about.

"What's Mr. Webber gonna do?" he asked instead.

"Goin' back to Minnesota with his other two kids and his brothers for now," Erik shrugged as he stared at Pioneer Peak. "Sad."

"Yeah," Paul followed his gaze. "Very sad."

The graves in the new little cemetery were adding up.

Chapter 26
A Sourdough Christmas

"Paul, wake up! Come on, it's Chwistmas!" Clara yelled as she tried to take his blankets off.

"Ugh." Paul rolled over and pulled the thick pile of quilts back over his head. Belle barked and wagged her tail as she stood beside the girls with her front legs up on the bed.

There had already been Christmas festivities for all the colonists at the new school gymnasium a few days earlier. Companies such as Sears Roebuck and Alaska Commercial Company had sent gifts north on a steamship. Santa was there to give each child a present, along with fruit and candy. It had been a joyful celebration as the colonists reunited with each other now that all were in their own homes.

"Paul! It's Chwistmas! Get up!"

Clara and Minnie pushed and poked at him until he finally sat up. He laughed at their faces, alight with excitement. It was cold enough inside the house that little clouds of frozen moisture hung in the air every time they spoke or breathed.

"Fire must have gone out," he mumbled as he rubbed his eyes. He heard Ma's voice coming from downstairs. "Better go help her get the fire started. Come on, Belle. Ma hates finding the fire out in the morning."

As they came down the stairs they stopped and stared in disbelief.

A Christmas tree stood in a corner of the small living room, propped up with wire, and decorated with lit candles. Underneath were several unwrapped gifts. A fire crackled in the stove.

126

Ma smiled as she stood in the kitchen doorway with a blanket wrapped around her shoulders, watching their faces. Pa was putting another log into the stove.

"Merry Christmas!" they said together.

The girls raced down the stairs, squealing with delight.

"How did all this happen?" Paul asked.

"Oh, Santa knows where we live, doesn't he, Pa?" Ma looked at Pa with a grin.

"Yes, except I think Mrs. Claus did most of it. Minnie, Clara, come away from those gifts. We're going to have breakfast first," said Pa. "In fact, we're going to have an Alaskan breakfast, with real sourdough hotcakes. And I'm going to make them!"

"You're going to cook, Pa?"

"Yep, believe it or not! Your Ma's been up since the wee hours of the morning so I'll cook. Where's your famous skillet, Mary?"

"I'll get more wood and water," Paul offered cheerfully as he went out the back door with Belle trotting behind.

"These pancakes are great, Pa," said Minnie as she stuffed another big piece dripping with syrup into her mouth. "Why do they call them sourdough?"

"They're made from sourdough starter that you save every time you make bread or pancakes." Ma explained. "Your Pa got this starter from an old miner. Tell them the story, Henry."

"Well, I was delivering wood up at Independence Gold Mine in Hatcher Pass a few days ago. Men have built big warehouses, a mess hall, and dorms up there in the mountains, and since there ain't no trees or mills up there, every stick of wood had to be hauled up. They've got mine shafts and rails for the cars to bring dirt out where it's washed to get at the gold. Pretty amazing. Pass me another hotcake, would ya Paul? I'll have to take you all up there some day."

Pa finished another hotcake, then pushed his plate back and patted his stomach. "Mighty fine." He took another swig of coffee. "Anyways, I got to talkin' to the cook one day about how they get their food up there and he mentioned sourdough hotcakes for breakfast every day and sometimes for dinner with meat and gravy on them."

"Eww, yuck," Clara scrunched up her nose.

"Well, said they're delicious and asked if I wanted a little starter to take home. Says this particular one came from a fella during the 1898 gold rush and it's been kept alive all these years. Imagine that— thirty seven years old!"

"Well, I'll take these for breakfast any day!" Paul said as he devoured two more, then leaned back and patted his stomach.

"Can we see the pwesents now?" Clara tugged on Pa's shirt sleeve.

"You bet, little missy. The fire finally warmed this place up. Shall we take our coffee into the living room and enjoy our new furniture, Mother?" he said with a twinkle in his eyes.

"That sounds lovely," said Ma with a big smile. A "finished" house and new furniture were all she needed for Christmas.

Minnie, the self-appointed elf, handed out the presents as everyone laughed and joked. Ma and Pa kissed when they opened theirs.

I can't remember the last time I saw Ma and Pa kiss! thought Paul.

"Play us a tune on the piano, Mary." Pa urged.

All afternoon the house brimmed with music and laughter as the family sang Christmas carols. Ham and potatoes were served for dinner, followed by blueberry pie and hand-churned ice cream.

This has been the best Christmas ever! Right out of a storybook! thought Paul, as he took one more serving of pie and ice cream.

Chapter 27
Fun at the Lake

"Francine! It seems like forever since I saw you last!" Maggie gave her a big hug. "How's your baby brother?"

They both found a large rock to sit on to fasten their skate blades to the bottom of their boots.

"Oh, he's getting so big! But, he still cries for hours every night!"

"That doesn't sound like much fun."

"Being quarantined at home for two weeks hasn't been fun either, has it?"

"Ugh! I never thought I'd say it, but I can't wait to go back to school on Monday! This smallpox epidemic is no fun!" Maggie sighed.

"Yeah, and I hear the nurse is giving us shots when we get back. Won't that be even more fun?"

"Mother said at least ten people have come down with it."

"That's horrible!"

Maggie finished with her skates, stood up, and promptly landed with a thud on her bottom. "Ouch, this ice is hard!"

Francine laughed. "I'll be right beside you in a minute. I haven't skated in a while, either."

"Well, not everyone's rusty. Those guys playing hockey on the other side of the lake are pretty good," Maggie said as she brushed herself off.

"Some of the men I came over with mentioned they were starting up a hockey team. Ouch!" Francine fell, too. "I can hardly stand up, much less play hockey!"

Maggie laughed as she helped Francine up.

They watched the skaters pass a puck back and forth for a minute before they realized Paul and Erik were two of the players. The girls waved and started over toward them.

"This is like a mirror, isn't it?" Francine giggled.

"This warm weather we've been having makes it perfect for skating. Father said it happens nearly every January, and the old-timers call it a chinook."

"Well, I like the snow better. I thought there'd be lots of it in Alaska! Now it's almost all melted." Francine glanced around as she tried not to fall. "How's your father doing?"

"He got the cast off a while ago, but he's still limping around and his toes get cold right away," Maggie sighed. "Said he'd love to come outside and play, but it'll be a while! Mother's here, though. She couldn't wait to come skating."

"Well, there she is," pointed Francine.

They watched as Mrs. Cooper skated with graceful strides, and then turned backwards, extending one of her legs in the air like a real figure skater.

"Wow, I didn't know your mother could skate like that!"

"Neither did I!" Maggie responded in awe.

"Hi there, you two," Paul skated toward them and did an abrupt hockey stop, showering them both with shaved ice.

"Stop showing off!" Maggie laughed, brushing the ice off. "I didn't know you two played hockey."

"Well, we're from Minnesota, aren't we?" Paul gave Erik a big shove with his shoulder, which sent him flying. "That's what we call a check, which is totally legal," Paul laughed as he helped Erik to his feet.

"At least give me a little warning next time," said Erik as he brushed the ice off his pants. Suddenly he hooked Paul's legs with the blade of his stick and pulled, sending Paul flying. "And that's what we call a hook, which is totally illegal."

"Okay, we're even," said Paul as he stood up. "Let's get back to some real hockey. See ya!" The boys checked each other playfully as they skated back toward the rest of the players.

As the afternoon passed, more and more people came out to enjoy Tomlinson Lake in the winter. Mr. Engles was ice-fishing in one corner. Reverend Bingle, who had brought Francine and others from the Butte, skated around the lake, happily chatting with everyone. Occasional cheers were heard from spectators watching the hockey scrimmage at the other end of the lake.

After a while, Maggie and Francine took a break to warm up with a mug of steaming hot cocoa by the campfire.

"Mmm. This is so yummy when you're cold, isn't it?" Maggie sipped her drink.

"Delicious." Francine suddenly pointed across the ice. "Look!"

A bald eagle perched high on the top of a spruce tree above Mr. Engles' fishing hole stealthily opened its massive wings and swooped down toward several small trout that lay in a row on the ice. Mr. Engles must have heard the whoosh of its wings, for he turned just in time to see the gigantic bird with a six-foot wingspan coming in his direction, and dove onto the ice.

Gracefully, the eagle picked up one of the fish in his talons and beat the air with slow, powerful thrusts of his wings. He returned to the tree and had his own afternoon snack while everyone watched in awe.

"Did you see that?" whispered Francine, though, of course every-one on the ice had witnessed it.

"Poor Mr. Engles!" said Maggie. "He must have nearly had a heart attack!"

"Well, he must not feel too bad, because he's already trying to catch another fish to make up for the eagles!" exclaimed Maggie's mother, who had come to warm up by the fire.

Everyone laughed and went back to their activities. As it grew dark, big fluffy snow-flakes started to fall. Minnie, Clara, and some younger children skated with their heads back, giggling as they tried to catch snowflakes with their tongues. Groups of people laughed and talked as they warmed cold hands around the fire. Several little boys picked up their father's hockey sticks and were clumsily trying to hit a puck around.

Maggie suddenly felt a violent tug as someone grabbed her hand and yanked her across the ice. It was Paul. Screaming and laughing, she found herself at the end of a line of skaters playing crack the whip.

"Help!" Maggie yelled playfully as she was whisked past Francine. The lead skater purposefully twisted and pulled the line faster and harder. Finally, the force of the whip was so strong, Maggie couldn't hold Paul's hand anymore. She flew across the ice, landing firmly in some willow bushes along the bank. She shivered as snow from the branches covered her head and settled down her neck.

"Are you alright?" Paul laughed as he held out his hand to help her up.

"I don't think I trust you!" she giggled playfully as she wiped wet snow off her face.

She took his hand to stand up and promptly pushed him into the same bushes, laughing as he sat covered in snow.

"That's what you call paybacks, which is totally legal!" she whooped and joked as Paul chased her back to the fire to warm up and have one last mug of cocoa.

"This has been so much fun," Francine said as they prepared to head home. "Why don't you ask your mother if you could come home with me and spend the night?"

"Oh, that's a swell idea! I'll be right back." Maggie ran to find Mother.

"I can come! Oh, I'm so excited!" she giggled as they climbed into Reverend Bingle's car to head back to the Butte. "We can stay up and talk, and look at clothes in the catalog …"

"And I'll catch you up on all the news with Andy and his gang," Francine said in a tone that told Maggie that she knew about his thievery. "And I learned a new game called Easy Money—it's so much fun!"

"And we can put each other's hair up in curlers …" and on and on it went all the way home to Francine's house.

"Hey, Paul," Erik waved his hand in front of Paul's face. "Are you there?"

Paul had been watching the car drive away with Maggie and Francine, and was deep in thought.

"Huh? Yea, course I'm here. What?"

"I was asking if you'd like to stay at my house tonight. We could look at clothes in the catalog, too!" he squeaked in a girl's voice.

Paul laughed. "And we could do each other's hair …" he squeaked back. "A hot sauna sounds a whole lot better!"

"You ready to try it again?" Erik was surprised.

"You bet! Now that I'm a real man!" he smiled. "Race ya back!"

Chapter 28
Winds

Paul had his routine for the cold days of winter. Ever since they had been in the tent he had two jobs each night: get kerosene for the lamps and wood for the stove. Being in the house was a slight improvement, but it was still cold enough to freeze water in the kettle during the night.

Every morning his job was first to light the lamp so he could see to light the stove. That would eventually thaw the water in the kettle, which he would carry out to the well house and pour on the pump to unfreeze it. Then he pumped water to take back inside for Ma, and watered the animals. He was pretty used to it, except when the winds blew off the glaciers and into the Matanuska Valley. Then it really got cold and the whole process seemed to take forever!

"Now, what could be taking them so long," Ma said aloud as she stood in the enclosed back porch, watching worriedly for Pa and Paul. She hugged a mug of steaming coffee close to her chest with one hand while she held her hand to the frosted window, trying to thaw a circle big enough to see out of.

"They'll be back, Ma," said Minnie as she washed the breakfast dishes. "You worry too much."

Ma glanced at her with a surpriscd look and Minnie smiled back affectionately. "Well, you do," she dried a cup and placed it in the cupboard. "And things always work out fine. They'll be back soon."

"My, my," sighed Ma. "Just when did you grow up?"

"Oh, while you weren't looking!" Minnie giggled as she finished and turned to run upstairs to find Clara.

"Well, you are right—here they come!"

"See?" Minnie popped her head back around the corner.

Ma smiled.

"Well, the animals are hanging in there," Pa said as he came in through the back door and laid an armful of wood on the floor by the stove. "Brrr. I've never felt cold like this before."

"It's that wind," answered Ma, taking Pa's hat and scarf as he removed layers of winter clothing.

"We had winds in Minnesota, too, if you remember," Pa said.

"For days at a time with wind chills to 30° and 40° below zero?"

"Well, things are pretty extreme up here, especially the long, dark days of winter. Kind of gets to you after a while if I say so myself."

"Really!" said Ma, somewhat sarcastically. Obviously Pa's words were an understatement for the way she had felt from the very beginning. "I take it the tent's still standing?"

"Barely! Hmmm, coffee sounds great," Pa rubbed his hands to warm them as Ma poured a cup from the blue enamel coffeepot on the stove. He peeked out the little circle of the frosted window that Ma had cleared. "Here he comes."

Paul had a bucket of steaming milk in one hand and icy cold water from the well in the other. His head was bent low against the wind. Belle trotted along behind him, her brown coat thick and fluffy for the winter, as if she didn't even notice that it was bitter cold out.

Pa held the door open to usher them both into the warmth of the house. Fine grains of snow, like sand, pelted him and swirled in the doorway. Ma took the bucket of milk while Belle shook off the snow and curled up behind the stove.

"Wow, sure glad they canceled school!" Paul stomped the snow off his boots. He set the water down next to the wood, took off his gloves, and breathed on his fingers to warm them. "Erik just stopped by to borrow a milk can and told me about the Larsh place. Is that alright if I lent him one, Pa?"

Pa nodded. "Sure, but what's he doin' out in weather like this? And what about the Larsh place?"

"When he's got news he has to share it no matter what the weather!" Paul laughed. "He told me the wind blew the roof clear off their house last night. Right while everyone was asleep!"

"Land sakes," Ma put her hands up to her face and involuntarily looked up to the ceiling. "It don't surprise me, the way they built these!"

She looked at Pa for reassurance.

"I helped build it, and this roof ain't goin' nowhere. I reckon the Larshes have about the windiest spot in the whole valley," he winked at Paul, hoping to sound convincing.

"So, what did they do? Are they alright?" Ma said, worried.

"Mr. Larsh ran to the neighbors who fetched them all in their horse-drawn sleigh and took them back for the night. Guess they'll be stayin' there till they can get the roof back on."

"Well, don't that beat all," murmured Pa, pouring one more cup of coffee. "I'll have to see if there's anything I can do to help once it calms down."

"How does Erik seem to know everything that goes on around here?" laughed Ma. "He's a regular telegraph station!"

"He does have a nose for news," Pa remarked. "Maybe he could get a job at the *Matanuska Pioneer*!"

"That's not a bad idea," Paul laughed. "I bet Mr. Allman could use a roving reporter!"

Everyone continued to comment about the poor Larsh family as they went about the morning.

Later that afternoon the winds died down and temperatures rose enough to go out. Ma and Pa set out on the quarter mile walk to the Coopers' place to find out more about the Larshes unfortunate situation. Neighbors visited neighbors nearly every day. On the way they passed Maggie and David who were pulling a wooden sled.

"Hi, Mr. and Mrs. Jacobs," David asked. "Is Paul home?"

"Sure is. Yer plannin' to go sleddin' I see," said Mr. Jacobs. "Do you mind if the girls go with you? We asked Paul to watch them for a while. Your folks at home?"

"Yep, they're both there," said David.

"And we'd love to bring the girls!" said Maggie, cheerfully.

Paul was sprawled on the living room floor in front of the coal-burning stove, flipping through the latest *Fur, Fish, and Game* magazine. Dreams of fishing trips and outdoor expeditions filled his head as he studied the pictures. Minnie and Clara played upstairs, making believe they were movie stars like the ones they had seen in the movies in San Fransisco.

He jumped when he heard a knock at the door.

"You up for some sledding?" David asked with a big grin.

"Sure, come on in!"

Maggie and David stepped inside the small arctic entryway.

"We're getting cabin fever!" laughed Maggie. "Figured with school being closed we might as well have some fun!"

"We just passed your folks," said David. "They asked if the girls could join us."

"Did you hear that, Minnie and Clara?" Paul yelled up to his sisters, whose beaming faces were peeking around the top of the stairs.

"Weady ow not, hew we come!" sang Clara, as they skipped down the stairs.

Snow pants, boots, coats, hats, and mittens were rounded up as they raced and tripped over each other to get ready for the cold. Soon, the little party was headed toward a steep bank nearby that led down to the frozen Matanuska River.

"Yippee," they laughed and screamed as they soared down through drifted mounds of fluffy snow and out onto the bumpy ice. Everyone laughed to see each other covered from head to toe with snow. It took two people, usually Paul and David, to pull the heavy sled back up the hill. They spent all afternoon sledding.

"My feet are cold," whined Clara.

"Mine, too," said Minnie.

"Let's go back for some cocoa and cake!" said Maggie. "I made a chocolate cake that's just begging to be eaten."

"Oh, we love cake!" Minnie cried. "Come on, Clara, I'll race ya to Maggie's house!"

They ran ahead laughing with delight.

"A cake that's beggin' to be eaten is my favorite kind!" Paul smiled at Maggie. *She's sure cute all bundled up, her cheeks rosy from the cold!*

Maggie blushed, then bent down to pick up some snow and threw it at Paul. The three threw snowballs and teased each other all the way back to Maggie's house.

"You know, we've almost made it through the winter," Paul said as he devoured a piece of cake.

"You're right," said Maggie. "It's already the first of March and the days are getting longer, now that you mention it."

"It doesn't look like winter's ready to leave any time soon," said David wryly.

"Well, when we got here last May it was definitely spring, so it's got to warm up eventually!" laughed Paul.

"Wow, hard to believe it'll be a year pretty soon. Sure have been a lot of changes from our old life back home," muttered David as he ate.

"I've loved nearly every minute of it!" said Maggie.

"That's because you're an eternal optimist!" David rolled his eyes. "You always think everything's wonderful!"

"Well, it's better to be that way than a 'negative Ned,' like Mother says." She tossed her long, brown hair over her shoulder.

"Well, I'd better get these girls home. Need to get some kerosene and wood ready for tomorrow or I'll be a 'pitiful Paul'!" he laughed as he called for the Minnie and Clara. "Thanks for the sledding and delicious cake—that was fun!" Paul winked at Maggie as he went out the door.

Maggie laughed and picked up the nearest thing she could find, a wet hat, and threw it at him but he closed the door just in time.

Chapter 29
Grandpa

Sun streamed in the classroom window of the Matanuska School.

"Paul, do tell the class what you're daydreaming about that's so much more interesting than school." Miss Adams stood over Paul, who turned red with embarrassment.

"I'm sorry, Miss Adams. Just thinkin' about fishin', I guess."

The other students snickered.

"Well, please try to pay attention or you'll miss something important." She walked back to the blackboard and wrote "Test tomorrow on the Civil War, Pages 11-25," but Paul was already back to looking out the window and didn't notice.

Though temperatures were still only in the teens, icicles dripped off the sides of the roof and the sun's rays felt warm on Paul's face as he walked out to the bus. No sooner had the bus dropped him off, than he and Belle were headed to Tomlinson Lake with ice pick, bucket, and fishing pole in hand. The lakes were still frozen solid—perfect for ice fishing.

A few hours and several fish later, Paul and Belle came in through the back door. He was all ready to show off his catch, when he sensed something wrong. It was too quiet. Was the tick-tock of the clock on the mantle too loud? Maybe it was the barely audible voices coming from behind Ma and Pa's closed bedroom door.

And why is food still cooking on the stove? Paul wondered. *Ma never does that.*

He took the food off the stove and crept closer to the bedroom door. Ma was sobbing in a muffled sort of way and Pa was speaking softly, which wasn't like him. Now Paul was worried.

He knocked on the door. "Ma, are you okay?" He opened it slightly.

Ma was standing, crying into Pa's chest as he embraced her. His cheek lay against her head and he gently swayed back and forth as if trying to console a baby.

"Gramps died, Paul. Last week. We just got the letter today." Pa's expression told him they needed some time alone.

Paul gently shut the door and leaned back against the wall of the hallway.

No! Poor Gramps. And Ma was planning to go back to visit this summer. And Gran. Have they already had his funeral and we didn't even know? Now what? I wonder what Ma's gonna do. His mind was spinning and grieving all at the same time. He loved Gramps.

Paul squatted down and quietly patted Belle's head. Tears ran down his cheeks. "Used to sit in the barn with Rascal during times like this, Belle-Belle. Wish we had a barn now," he sighed. He wiped the tears from his face. "Better go check on dinner."

Ma didn't come out of her room all evening. The others ate solemnly and cleaned up the kitchen in silence. The girls tiptoed upstairs to whisper back and forth about Gramps and what death must be like. Minnie cried off and on because she could remember more, and then Clara cried because Minnie was crying.

Pa sat pensively in the overstuffed chair by the stove, puffing on his pipe.

"What do you think Ma's gonna do?" Paul asked as he sat cross-legged on the floor looking at the big photo album.

"Don't rightly know," Pa said, staring at a corner of the ceiling as if deep in thought. "Don't really have the money to send her home quite yet." He tamped the bowl of the pipe and lit the tobacco again, a common ritual when Pa smoked his pipe. He took another few puffs. "Then again, she may just want to move back for good," he sighed. "Wouldn't that beat all. Sixty-three families done left last I heard."

Pa's thinkin' the same thing I'm thinkin'. But Paul didn't say anything.

"Bad day at the sawmill today, too. Man died—fell under the blade. Terrible." He paused. "Don't want to tell your Ma 'bout that.

139

News'll get around, though." He got up and opened the bin of the stove to throw in more coal.

"Was it someone we knew?"

"Not very well. Fella from the Butte."

Five minutes went by before he finally spoke again. "They say bad things come in threes. Wonder what the third thing'll be."

"That's just superstition, Pa. It's better to think positive." Paul thought of Maggie.

"Hmmm, we'll see."

"Look, there's you and Gramps and Uncle Will with the deer Gramps shot," Paul held up the picture for Pa to see. "Wasn't that when Uncle Will almost shot you?"

"Yep, that was a close one. Your Ma's brother never was too handy with a gun. But Gramps was another story. He was quite a shot." He bent over to look at the picture. "That was the biggest buck he ever took."

Paul slowly flipped through the pages of the photo album while Pa sat in silence for a long time.

"Well," he finally muttered. "Got to be at the mill early so think I'll turn in. Good night." He looked at Paul for the first time, went into the bedroom, and closed the door.

Ma was up making breakfast the next morning, quietly going about her daily routine. Pa had left long ago, catching a ride with the only neighbor who had a truck. Ma never mentioned Gramps or what she might do, though her eyes were still red and puffy from crying all night. Paul and the girls kissed her goodbye as they went out to catch the schoolbus.

Paul hesitated before he shut the door and looked back at Ma. She caught his glance.

"I'll let you know tonight," she smiled knowingly, as if reading his thoughts.

Miss Adams was standing beside her desk when Paul walked into class. "Good morning, students. Please have a seat and take out a pencil for our test on the Civil War. I hope you all studied last night," she smiled.

Paul sat up straight. *Oh, no! What test?*

Chapter 30
The Last Straw

"Okay, Maggie May. We better get moving or we'll miss the Brill Car into Anchorage," Father kissed her forehead. "Should be back late afternoon. The list is on the table. Try to get as much done as you can."

"Have a good time," she waved.

The Brill Car was a long car that had been transformed into a rail car. It held ten passengers, and zipped along the railroad tracks to Anchorage and back once a day.

"Ugh, chores!" She sighed as she studied the list. "Let's see. First I better milk Darlene, then I'll start the ironing."

"Yep, they never end, do they?" David said as he bounded down the stairs. "At least we don't have to work at a real job like Michael. He might as well live up at the mine since he's never home anymore." He put on some leather gloves and a coat. "I better get more firewood split. Those are pretty dark clouds out there." He whistled as he headed for the woodpile.

Maggie walked out to Darlene's tent, studying the clouds that spit cold drops of rain. By the time she'd finished milking, the rain had turned to huge wet flakes of snow that covered everything. They swished this way and that with the wind as she carried the steaming milk pail up to the house.

"The weather can't make up its mind between winter and spring!" she called to David. "Is April always like this in the north?"

"I reckon so," he answered as he raised his maul to split another piece of wood.

Once inside, she filled the chamber of the new iron with fuel, pumped it several times, and lit the little burner underneath. While it heated, she put a record of Glen Miller's big band music on the phonograph in the living room and cranked up the volume. One by one the clothes in the basket were hung up, clean and crisply ironed.

"Too bad Francine's not here—she would have enjoyed this more than I do!" she said to herself, smiling. "At least it's more fun to work to music!"

"Bake a cake and scrub the floors are all that's left," she read. "Well, guess I'll do the floors while the cake is baking. Better stoke the fire first." She put a pail of water on the stove, and threw a few pieces of wood into the bin. Humming along to music of Benny Goodman and Louis Armstrong, she mixed the cake ingredients and placed the pans gently in the oven.

When the water in the pail was warm, Maggie got down on hands and knees to scrub the kitchen floor with soapy water and a bristle brush. The cake timer dinged just as she finished, her face flushed and arms tired with the effort.

"That was good timing!" she brushed a strand of hair out of her face and sat back on her heels. "I'm tired!"

"Me, too!" said David, who had just come in through the back door with an armload of wood.

"Don't get the floor dirty! I just washed it!"

"Oops!"

"Ugh! Brothers!"

"Well, I'll be out of your hair for a while. Goin' huntin." He jumped off the back steps with a shotgun over his shoulder and a big smile on his face.

Finally done, Maggie poured a glass of milk and plunked down on the sofa to rest. The April 1936 edition of *Time Magazine,* with a picture of a man named Adolph Hitler on the cover, caught her attention. "Wonder who he is," she murmured. She flipped through a few pages but traded it for the spring/summer edition of the Montgomery Ward's catalog.

"That was quite a ride home," exclaimed Father as he and Mother returned from Anchorage. "It's snowing like crazy. Nothing like a snowstorm this time of year! Wonder if Michael will make it home."

"I've been worried about you all," said Maggie.

A while later the back door opened. David set his shotgun in the corner of the porch and proudly held up two brown and white birds.

"And look who else I found out ptarmigan hunting!"

"Hi there," Paul smiled as he followed David in, holding up three birds. "Supper! Pretty easy to spot them in the snow this time of year."

"Come in," welcomed Father. "Good job, boys. Say, we heard something about your mother on the Brill Car into Anchorage today and wondered if it was true."

"What do you mean, Father? What did you hear?" Maggie looked at Paul.

Paul glanced back, hung the string of birds up on a hook outside the back door, and stepped inside.

There was an uncomfortable silence as Maggie, Father, and David stood looking at Paul, waiting to hear the news.

"Poor boy!" scolded Mother as she came out of the kitchen. "Let him come in and warm up first. Goodness, putting him on the spot like that!"

Paul held a hot mug of tea as they sat in the living room while he started his story.

"We got a letter two days ago saying Gramps, Ma's Papa, had passed away a week ago. He hasn't been well for a while. She took it pretty hard, but went into Palmer yesterday and talked to Gran on the phone from the telegraph office. Said she was gonna go back to Minnesota in June, and they would have Gramps' funeral then."

"We're sorry to hear that, Paul," said Mother.

"Well, this afternoon when she saw the snow, something seemed to snap. She got her suitcase out and started packing. Said she was leaving on the morning train and gonna take Clara with her. She needed to see Gran. Said she had to get out of here—just couldn't take it anymore. Didn't know if she would come back." He took a sip of his tea and was silent for a moment. "I decided to go huntin' and not think about it for a while. Reckon there will have been some decision by the time I get back. Pa should be home from the sawmill by now. He said bad things happen in threes. Guess this is number three." He looked up. "This here is home for me now."

"Paul, why don't I go back to your place with you and see if I can be of any help," said Father, rising to get his coat.

"I'll go, too," said David.

By evening Father and David still hadn't returned.

"Sure wish we had phones, like back in Michigan," said Maggie wistfully. "This waiting and not knowing is torture!"

"I'm sure they're fine," Mother tried to sound encouraging. "They'll be back any time." But she looked out the window every few minutes with a worried gaze as the snow continued to blow and make deep drifts around the house. Finally, it was too dark to see.

Maggie rubbed her eyes. "Well, it's almost midnight. Guess I'll turn in. Good night, Mother," she kissed her cheek. Snuggled under the quilt, she got out her diary:

> Dear Diary,
> Lots happened today. Chores, chores, chores. Never end, but it's a good feeling. Paul stopped by and told how his mother might leave for Minnesota with Clara and not come back. Is it a coincidence that the Minnesota colonists left for Alaska exactly one year ago today? If the Jacobses go back it'll never be the same. I would be heartbroken! Wonder what the morning will bring besides lots of snow! So tired!
> Love, Maggie

Maggie didn't have to wait until morning. Sometime in the middle of the night, she heard Father and David return and ran downstairs, wide awake.

"What happened?" she cried.

"What a night!" exclaimed Father as he brushed the snow off his coat. He looked very tired. "Everyone's alright, thank goodness."

He and David stood over the stove rubbing their hands together to warm up.

"Found out Michael stayed with some friends in town after work when he saw the snow."

"I figured as much," said Mother. "But do tell us about Mary. We're dying to know!"

"Well, the snow was the last straw for Mary, and like Paul said, she packed her and Clara's bags to leave. When Henry got home he tried everything he could think of to convince her to think it through but the more he tried the more determined she was to go. They actually got into a pretty heated argument, so she decided she would leave right then and there, without Clara. Well, everyone was very upset, especially the girls, as you can imagine."

"She must be overwhelmed with grief," sighed Mother sympathetically.

"Anyway, by the time we got there, she had hitched Fannie up to the wagon and was trying to leave for the train station. In the dark!"

"There aren't any trains that leave at night, are there?" asked Maggie.

"No, of course not," said Father. "But no one could talk any sense into her, short of tying her down! Henry threw up his hands and said 'Let her go if she's so stubborn!' and off she went!"

"Unbelievable!" said Mother softly.

"Henry figured she'd realize how foolish it was to be heading to the train station when there isn't a train, especially in a snowstorm. So we waited, but she never did come back."

"Oh, my!" said Mother

"Then, of course, we got worried and started to think of all the things that could happen. Had she gone off the road and gotten stuck in a snowbank? Would we be able to find her? Might she freeze to death out there somewhere?" Father finally sat down in his favorite chair to continue the story.

"David, thank goodness, offered to run over to the Engleses' place and borrow their horse to go look for her. Sure enough, almost two hours later there she was, sitting alone on a little bench at the station, all by herself in the snow and darkness. There weren't even any lights on!"

"Oh dear!" muttered Mother. "That's terrible! Then what did you do, David?"

"I took her to Doc Albrecht's. By the time I found her she was shivering and kind of in shock. I figured the hospital would be the safest place since she definitely did not want to go back home."

"Bless your heart," Mother smiled at David.

"Doc said he'd watch her overnight, which was a great relief considering her state of mind!" added Father. "It was terrible waiting all that time and not knowing if David had found her or not. But, all's well that ends well, at least for tonight!" He yawned.

"Goodness, I wonder what'll happen now?" said Maggie.

"Henry and I had lots of time to talk while we waited. He'll have to see how she is in the morning, but he sure doesn't want to move out of Alaska. Well, I'm going to bed. I'm exhausted, aren't you, David?"

"I sure am. Good night."

Maggie and Mother lingered in the kitchen for a while, too keyed up to sleep.

"What if Henry lets her go home and she never comes back?" wondered Maggie.

"I don't think she'd do that," said Mother.

"She wouldn't leave her children, would she?"

"Well, I won't name names but another woman did just that. Left her husband and four kids! But I think it'll all work out okay."

"Oh, you're always so positive, Mother!"

"Well, what good does it do to be negative and think the worst? Things always work out with time," Mother smiled.

Maggie yawned. Mother bent down to kiss her on the cheek.

"We'll see what happens tomorrow. At least Mary's safe in the hospital. We better get our beauty sleep! Good night!"

"Good night," said Maggie as she slowly went upstairs and crawled back under her quilt. She was asleep in two seconds.

Chapter 31
Homecoming

Spring thaws and occasional rains on the newly built roads left mud and muck. Canada geese, ducks, swans, and sandhill cranes filled the skies with honking and whirring as they migrated back north in noisy, giant Vs. Wild geraniums and chiming bells bloomed in the woods. Mosquitoes buzzed and bit. Days of May were long, the sun was warm, trees were leafing out, and the world was full of new life.

Fannie stopped at the edge of the huge mud puddle flooding Springer Road. Pa slapped the reins on her rump and prompted her across, hesitantly, with water rising halfway up the wagon wheels. The little family sat quietly as the wagon jostled and bounced along.

Ma had left alone for Minnesota a week after "the episode," and Pa, Paul, and his sisters remembered the trip to the station to watch her leave, not sure if or when she would come back. It had been a difficult month. No one realized just how many things Ma took care of at home until she was gone. Pa had let them all stay home from school as they headed back to the station to pick her up. Her letter had been brief:

> Have missed you all very much. My train comes in May 13th at 11:30 a.m. Hope you can pick me up then.
>
> Love, Mary

Pa pulled his pocket watch out and checked the time. "It's due in any time," he said, as he pulled Fannie to a stop. They all looked down the tracks for a sign. Belle heard the train first and started barking

"Is that it?" Paul asked Belle, patting her on the back. "Yep, there she comes." His thoughts were jumbled. *I wonder what this will be like. Will she be happy to be back up here, or will she take one look and pack up everything and go back for good? Will she even be on the train?*

Even Pa seemed a little nervous. Minnie and Clara stood next to him quietly as he sat on the bench seat of the wagon. Pa had his arms around them, as if they were all holding their breaths and each other to see whether Ma would step off the train.

The brakes screeched and the whistle blew. It seemed to take forever for the wheels to finally stop and the doors to open. By now everyone was standing beside the wagon and searching the cars for a sign of Ma.

"There she is!" cried Minnie, pointing to a face looking out the window of the third car. Ma was waving wildly, wearing a big hat and an even bigger smile.

Cheers went up from the family as the girls danced with joy. Pa breathed a sigh of relief, and Paul hugged Belle who jumped up and down gleefully as if understanding the importance of the whole event. Still, it seemed to take Ma a long time to leave the train. Who was she so busy talking to? Finally Ma appeared in the doorway, loaded with boxes and suitcases.

I forgot how pretty Ma is when she's all dressed up and smiling! Paul noticed.

"Hello, dears!" she laughed and hugged everyone. "Oh, it's so good to see you all. Wait now, I have a surprise." She handed her baggage to Pa, kissed him, and returned up the steps of the railcar. A few moments later she reappeared, helping someone down the steps.

"Gran!" they all shouted. "Oh, it's Gran, too!" Everyone hugged her and started talking and asking questions all at the same time.

It was Paul who noticed a small scraggly brown dog quietly trot down the stairs behind them.

"Rascal? Ma, you brought Rascal with you, too?" Paul got down on his knees and hugged her while Belle barked and wagged her tail with excitement. Rascal wriggled and squirmed with joy as she licked Paul's face. The girls jumped and danced gleefully.

When everyone had calmed down enough to catch their breath, they looked at Ma, who had been watching the reaction of her family. Tears streamed down her face.

"I missed you all so much, and I realized some very important things while I was back in Minnesota," she started. "First, my family is here now, and especially with Gran staying with us, this is home. Henry, I meant to talk with you about Gran before now, but I knew you'd approve." She looked at him sheepishly. "I missed you all so much, and I missed the mountains. I realize how absolutely gorgeous the Matanuska Valley is, isn't it, Gran?"

They both looked around at the huge mountains. "I never knew there was such a world as this out there," Gran spoke for the first time. "That was an unforgettable journey all the way up here, and it's as wonderful as your Ma said."

"Yes, and thank heavens the boat ride was much calmer this time!" Ma laughed. "Well, it's about time for lunch and Gran and I are starving. What say we head home and see what we can round up."

She had the girls sit beside her in the wagon, asking all sorts of questions: did Pa feed them decent, what's the weather been like, when did the mosquitoes come back, and what's new with the neighbors? Paul asked Gran about his cousins and what had been happening in Minnesota since they left. Pa whistled all the way home, occasionally adding a comment here and there. Belle and Rascal sniffed each other at first, but Rascal was tired and lay down for the wagon ride home.

Life settled in. Pa made the little room off the living room into a bedroom for Gran. Ma laughed and was happier. She often played the piano at church, and took Gran to her homemakers meetings every week. Men in the neighborhood got busy with the hard work of clearing, and helping each other get barns, chicken coops, and sheds built. The only style barn chosen by ARRC for all the colonists proved to be too small and not very sturdy, but at least it was a barn for the animals, equipment, and storage.

The great race was on to get land cleared and ready to use before next winter set in. Trees that had been slashed during the winter months were stacked, and stumps prepared to be pulled. Smoke from long rows of burning brush lingered like a veil over the valley.

One day Ma took advantage of the burn piles. "Minnie, take these potatoes out near the burn area to bake for dinner. And do be careful not to fall through the tundra!" Ma instructed. "Remember the poor Adams boy last summer!"

"Yes Ma."

"And don't forget where you buried them!"

"I won't, Ma."

One beautiful day Gran found a shovel and was planting a bush under the kitchen window. Paul and Minnie were busy pulling roots to make the family garden and overheard the conversation between Clara and Gran.

"Watcha doin?" asked Clara as she stood watching Gran dig in the silty soil.

"Plantin' a little lilac that I brought all the way from Minnesota."

"Why?"

"Because it'll be a beautiful tree some day, with pretty purple blooms."

"That's nice. But why wight thewe?"

"So it will smell nice through the kitchen window when it blooms," Gran smiled. "And I hope you'll think of me every time you smell the lilac blossoms."

"I pwomise I will!" Clara gave her a hug.

"And so will I," whispered Minnie to Paul as she bent over to pull another of the never-ending roots.

"Me, too," Paul mumbled under his breath as he watched Gran. "Me, too."

Chapter 32
Colony Days
May 16, 1936.

Cheering parents and ARRC officials lined the dirt road as children paraded past. First the youngest, on tricycles or riding in wagons pulled by other children, waved to the crowds. Grouped by age, dozens and dozens of children strolled, skipped, and cartwheeled proudly past their audience as they celebrated the anniversary of the colonists arrival. Paul, Erik, and Maggie laughed and waved cheerfully when they spotted their parents. The youngsters were the whole parade. After the oldest teens had passed, the crowds of adults fell in behind, greeting each other warmly.

"Hi there, Helen!"

"Hello, Mary!"

The women met, joined arms, and walked toward the other colonists gathered near the new Central School for the first Colony Days celebration as they caught up on news.

Buses, ARRC trucks, and horse-drawn wagons unloaded families in the town that hadn't even existed a year ago. The new water tower stood sentinel over the new railroad depot, a hospital, warehouses, the commissary, a garage, a power plant, and nearly two hundred homes for colonists and project officials.

Everyone sat on benches as they enjoyed lunch and listened to speeches. Various important people offered congratulations to the colonists for not giving up despite many odds. The weather even cooperated with sunshine and a breeze to help keep mosquitoes away.

"Come on, Clara," Minnie pulled Clara by the hand toward several tall, upright poles that had been placed in the ground. "It's time for the May Pole dance!"

Little girls in pretty dresses skipped, laughed, and sang as they wove and wrapped long ribbons around the poles.

Maggie, Francine, Paul, and Erik sat off to the side on a blanket, watching Paul's sisters dance.

"Remember standing at the train station a year ago when we were just starting out for Alaska?" said Maggie. "It was very exciting, though a little scary, don't you think?"

Paul nodded, but wouldn't admit to being scared out loud. "Wish I still fit in my leather jacket!" he laughed.

"I wonder how all our friends are doing back there," said Francine.

"I don't know, but I sure like my new friends up here!" Paul smiled with a twinkle in his eye.

"Me, too!" said Maggie and Erik together.

"Sometimes I wonder about all the families that left and ended up in Seattle or San Fransisco," said Paul.

"You sure can tell there's a lot fewer of us than there were at the beginnin'," said Erik, looking around.

"I remember standin' on the ship as it left San Fransisco and Pa sayin' lots would leave," Paul reminisced. "He also said it would take hard work and perseverance to make it."

"Well, he was right about both things," smiled Maggie. Her green eyes shone bright in the sunshine.

"I have a feeling the hard work part isn't over yet," laughed Erik.

"I think it's just begun!" replied Paul.

"Ugh! Chores, chores, chores!" said Maggie emphatically, throwing little pebbles across the ground.

"I reckon I'll be taking care of baby brothers and sisters my whole life," laughed Francine, who noticed her mother needing help with the baby. "See you guys later!" she waved as she headed over to her family.

"Yep, there's going to be gardens to plant and weed, cows to milk, animals to take care of, land to clear, fences to put up, wood to split, roots to pull and, oh yes …" Paul hesitated.

"Water to haul!" Paul and Erik said together, laughing.

"Hey, speaking of all that, are you guys busy doing chores later today?" Erik's grin told them he had a plan.

"Pa's taking the day off from working on the barn," said Paul.

"And Mother and Father are going visiting, so I'm free," said Maggie.

"Why?" they both asked together, eager to hear what he had in mind.

"I heard about this great fishing hole, and the monster fish are back—"

"I'm in!" shouted Paul.

"Me, too!" laughed Maggie. "As soon as the celebration is over, let's meet at your place, Erik!"

"Okay, but right now I'm still hungry. Let's go get some more food!" Erik jumped up and the others followed as they disappeared into the crowd.

By midafternoon people were making their way back to various neighbors' homes to visit, relax, and reminisce about the previous year.

Maggie and Paul arrived at Erik's house about the same time and were surprised to see an old friend sitting on the porch talking to Erik.

"Sam!" Maggie cried. "What are you doing here?"

"Oh, I've been eager to show you cheechakos a few secret fishing holes, especially since Erik told me what great fishermen you all are!"

"What's a cheeckako?" said Paul, "though I'm afraid to ask!"

"That's someone new to Alaska, who doesn't know a thing about how to survive up here in the north country!" Sam laughed.

"Well, I'd say we've learned a thing or two, and haven't done too awful bad at survivin' this past year, don't you think, Paul?" answered Erik.

"Yeah, I'd agree. Haven't we passed the test yet?" Paul wondered, jokingly.

"Well, I can't say yer sourdoughs yet, but it sounds like you sure are gettin' there!" Sam said with a smile.

"So, what are we waiting for? Let's get going!" exclaimed Maggie.

They all laughed and joked as the four, along with Belle and Rascal, headed through woods, across rivers, and over tundra in a new direction to discover yet another secret fishing hole and another adventure in this new land they called home.

Epilogue

Paul and Erik stood together quietly at the corner of Paul's old home-site and Springer Road. The sun was warm on their backs. Pioneer Peak stood as majestic as ever, its upper peak glistening with snow, its base green with the new life of spruce and birch. A mosquito biting his forearm caused Paul to look down and smile as he smacked it.

"Time hasn't changed everything!" he laughed.

"No, the mosquitoes will always be here," chuckled Erik softly, leaning on his cane.

"The old place sure isn't the same. Lots of homesites subdivided now."

"Yep. Our barn collapsed years ago. Just not the same without the barn," Erik shook his head sadly.

"Nope," Paul agreed. "Ours is still standing, barely. Spent many hours thinkin' 'bout life in that barn."

Silence.

"Your sauna's still standin'."

"That's because Pa knew how to build a sauna!" said Erik. "Remember your first sauna?"

"Unfortunately," Paul nodded slowly. "I'll never forget it!"

They both laughed for a moment.

Silence.

"There's the old lilac Gran planted. Scraggly, but still alive." Paul nodded toward the old house. "Loved the smell out the kitchen window."

"Yep. They've let the weeds take over, but it's still there."

"The pumphouse. Remember all the buckets of water? Too many to count all those years!"

"And kerosene lamps? Didn't get electricity till '42."

Silence.

"Seventy-five years ago. Wish Maggie was still here to celebrate."

"Yeah. She'd have loved seein' everyone again."

"We had a good life together. Four kids. Lots of wonderful memories." Paul wiped a tear from his weathered face. "Kind a hittin' me, ya know? Thinkin' about that first year up here, and all the things that happened. What a time."

"Think our kids and grandkids'll ever appreciate it?"

"I've tried to tell mine, but they're not too interested."

"Mine either."

Silence.

"Hopefully, they will some day."

Silence.

"Ready to go to the reunion picnic?"

"Yep. Let's go see who's still kickin'. Then maybe we can head out to Jim Creek and go fishin' for old times' sake," Erik grinned.

"There's a pretty good road out there now."

"Yep, a pretty good road. No more bushwackin' through devil's club."

"That's okay, my legs wouldn't take it anyway. Dang hip gives me problems."

"Yep, arthritis gets to me …"

Paul and Erik stood quietly for a while longer, each deep in thought with memories of a life long past.

Finally, hesitantly, they hobbled back to the car and made their way to the fairgrounds to celebrate with other colony kids whose bonds were forged through an experience as unique as the land itself. Alaska.

Bibliography

Alaska Far Away. Documentary. Juster Hill Productions, 2008.

Atwood, Evangeline. *We shall be remembered.* The Alaska Methodist University Press, Anchorage, Alaska, 1966

Cole, Vickie et al. *Knik, Matanuska, Susitna: A visual history of the valleys.* Brentwood Press, Sutton, Alaska, 1985

Gwin, Sally. *Mosquito Girl.* Royal Fireworks Press, Unionville NY, 1997

Harrier, J.J. *Settlers find a better life in the Valley. Frontiersman* 27 June 2008, sec C2.

Harrier, J.J. *Cultivating culture: Colony Days captures the history, growth of Palmer.*

Frontiersman 5 June 2009, Colony Days insert.

Irwin, Don. *The Colorful Matanuska Valley.* Don Irwin, 1968

Johnson, Greg. *Picturing the past: Scrapbook takes readers back to Colony days.*

Frontiersman 11 June 2010, sec A9

Johnson, Hugh A., and Keith L Stanton. *Matanuska Valley Memoir.* University of Alaska,

Alaska Experiment Station. Mapmakers Printing, Palmer, Alaska, 1980

Jordan, Nancy. *Frontier Physician. The life and Legacy of Dr. C. Earl Albrecht.* Epicenter Press, Fairbanks/Seattle, 1996

Lehn, Lynette A., and Lorraine M. Kirker. *Matanuska Colony 75th Anniversary Scrapbook.* Lehn & Kirker, 2010

Lively, Brigitte. *Matanuska Colony: Fifty Years, 1935-1985.* Matanuska Impressions Printing, 1985

Lively, Brigitte. *Matanuska Colony: Sixty Years. The colonists and their legacy.* Colony 60th Anniversary

Lundberg, Murray. "The Matanuska Colony: The New Deal in Alaska." www.explorenorth.com/library/yafeatures/bl-matanuska.htm

Matanuska Colony. Frontiersman, 11-13 June 2010. 75th Colony Days insert.

Matanuska Valley Colony Project 2010-2011 75th Anniversary Pictorial Calendar.

Miller, Orlando W. *The frontier in Alaska and the Matanuska colony.* Yale University Press, New Haven and London, 1975

Original Valley colonist injured in fall. Frontiersman 5 June 2009, sec A3.

Orth, Donald J. *Dictionary of Alaska Place Names.* United States Government Printing Office, Washington, 1971

Rebarchek, Ray as told to Robert L Tucker. *Memoirs of an Alaskan farmer.* Vantage Press, NY, 1980

Settlers in the Mat-Su Valley from Knik to Palmer in 1915. Knik News. 6 March 1915

Smitter, Wessel. *Another morning.* Harper & Brothers, NY, 1941

Where the River Matanuska Flows: Stories from Alaska Pioneers. Documentary/Memoirs. Juster Hill Productions, 2005. 180 min.

White, Rindi. *Original Colonist recalls early days. Anchorage Daily News* 11 June 2010, Sec A-12.

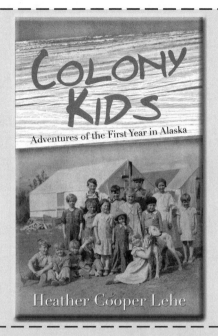

Use this Coupon to Order Additional Copies

Please ship to:

First Name _____ *Last Name* _____

Address _____

City _____ *State* _____ *Zip* _____

Phone Number _____ *email* _____

Orders shipped via Air Mail the day they are received.		Quantity	Total
	Colony Kids $14.95 each	_____	$ _____
	Shipping and Handling 3.00 each		$ _____
	No S and H with purchase **Grand Total** of two books or more.		$ _____

Credit Card Number _____ ❑ VISA

Expiration Date _____ Signature _____ ❑ MC

Publication Consultants

8370 Eleusis Drive, Anchorage, Alaska 99502
phone: (907) 349-2424 • fax: (907) 349-2426
www.publicationconsultants.com — email: books@publicationconsultants.com